# Monte Etna's Children

## A Story of Sicilian Immigration to America

# Monte Etna's Children

## A Story of Sicilian Immigration to America

## Monti-Gianino Family History and Genealogy

# Mary Linda Miller

mary linda miller
Orlando, Florida
www.marylindamiller.com

Cover design, inside cover, page layout, and graphic design by Mary Linda Miller © 2003, 2009, and 2010.

Cover and inside cover photograph: Family portrait of Eligio Monti with wife Sebastiana and nine children circa 1922 or 1923 by unknown photographer courtesy of the Milda (Kaempfe) Monti Estate.
Four boys standing on the left: Dominic (Don), Carmelo, Joseph (Joe), and Salvatore (Sam) Monti
Seated: Eligio Louis Monti with Little Frankie on his lap
Standing: Sebastiana (Gianino) Monti
Three girls standing on the right: Dominica Marie (Babe), Josephine (Josie), and Marie Margaret (Mary) Monti
Boy standing in foreground: Sebastiano (Charles) Joseph Monti

*Library of Congress* Cataloging Information
LC Control Number 2012371273

Miller, Mary Linda 1947—
    Monte Etna's Children: A Story of Sicilian Immigration to America
    Monti-Gianino Family History and Genealogy
    Mary Linda Miller, Orlando, Fla, © 2011

    viii, 86 p. : ill., maps; 26 cm.
    Includes bibliographical references (p. 63-66) and index.
    1. Monte family. 2. Italian Americans--Missouri--Saint Louis--Genealogy. 3. St. Louis (Mo.)—
    Genealogy.
CS71.M768 2011 OVERFLOWA5S          RG 929.20973 MONTI-GIANINO
ISBN-13: 9781463746704 (softcover)
ISBN-10: 1463746709 (softcover)

ISBN-10: 1463746709
ISBN-13: 978-1463746704
Published in the U.S.A.
Mary Linda Miller
Orlando, Florida
www.marylindamiller.com

# Dedication

For Mel and Jason
My sweethearts

Mount Sinai was covered with smoke, because the Lord descended on it in fire. The smoke billowed up from it like smoke from a furnace, the whole mountain trembled violently, and the sound of the trumpet grew louder and louder. Then Moses spoke and the voice of God answered him.

*Exodus 19: 18-19*

# Disclaimer

Large portions of the text and many illustrations, maps and photographs appeared in a 53-page booklet titled "The Genealogy of Carmelo Louis Monti and His Ancestral History" by Mary Linda Miller Each of the original eight limited edition copies bore the names of each of his five siblings or two parents in lieu of his name, and they were published on © September 11, 2003; subsequent partial photocopies were distributed to select family members in 2003 or thereafter; but the booklet was never offered for sale to the public. This new book represents a considerable revision to that material, in part because it focuses on only one of Carmelo's parent's ancestry. It includes numerous corrections, substantial new text, additional illustrations and photographs, and a revised descendants chart.

I make no guarantees that the material contained herein is accurate or complete, although I did attempt to make it so. Errors abound in the documents I obtained, especially spelling errors and conflicting dates. Many names and dates were provided to me in the form of handwritten notes or were the product of other genealogists' research; although I have verified many, others have not been or cannot be documented. Recollections, even eyewitness accounts, by a variety of living people conflicted with other versions of the same story from other sources, whether people, books, Internet, or newspapers. I weighed the variations and chose the one that seemed most plausible, and in many places I indicate where that happens. I have used the words "maybe" or "probably" or "likely" to indicate various levels of speculation, all my subjective opinion.

At any generation level there could be children not shown because they were not documented in anything available to me. Living persons' data has been reduced to "name only" for their privacy. The author specifically disclaims any responsibility for any liabilities, loss, or risk, personal or otherwise, which is incurred as a consequence, directly or indirectly, of the use and application of any of the contents of this book.

# Acknowledgments

Researching and writing this was a great adventure, but I could not have done it without help. Thanks are in order to numerous people.

1. Milda (Kaempfe) Monti for writing down many names and dates in 1986 and mailing it to her son Carmelo in Phoenix, Arizona, and for starting me on this journey.

2. Carmelo L. Monti, my husband, for contributing numerous drawings of maps, the illustration of Monte Etna; and for his advice on the cover and page design.

3. A special note of thanks to Sheila Monti-Molina for handling the photographs for the Milda (Kaempfe) Monti Estate and for making copies and distributing them to family members.

4. Others who have provided names, dates, photographs, or other material include Sheila Monti-Molina, Charlie Monti Jr., Paul Monti, Robert Willis, Louis C. Monti, Jill Palmer, Erin Farabee, Frank Monti, Roy Monti, Vera Monti, Victoria Monti, Sam Gianino, Tom and Joyce Beishir, Sharon Egler, Debbie Hadican, and Katie from Findagrave.com.

5. My son Jason Monti for solving my computer problems and for teaching me so many new things.

6. All of the sources in my bibliography, from which this document is derived.

# Table of Contents

Map of Sicily............................................................ viii

**Introduction**............................................................ 1

    Illustration: Monte Etna, Sicily, Italy............................ 2

**1. Ancient and Emigration History of Eligio Monte and Gianino Family Members**   3

    Birth Record for Eligio Monte................................. 5

    Marriage Record for Eligio Monte and Sebastiana Gianino.............. 6

    Photograph: Eligio and Sebastiana (Gianino) Monti c. 1922-23.......... 7

    Photograph: Ellis Island, New York c. 1913...................... 8

    Document: 1920 United States Census for St. Louis, Missouri........... 11

    Photographs: Feast of St. Domenic Parade Along Hale Street, Boston, MA .. 12

**2. The Gianino Family in Boston**.................................... 13

    Maps: West End Neighborhood in Boston and The Hill in St. Louis....... 15

    Photograph: The Family of Eligio and Sebastiana (Gianino) Monti........ 16

**3. Post-Emigration History in St. Louis, Missouri**...................... 17

    Photograph: Santa (Gianino) Gianino 1951....................... 17

    Photograph: Carmelo and Santa (Gianino) Gianino................. 18

    Photograph: Headstone for Carmelo and Santa Gianino.............. 19

    Photograph: An Early Monti Residence.......................... 20

    Document: Alien Registration Form for Eligio Monti................ 21

    Photograph: Eligio Luigi Monte a.k.a. Eligio Louis Monti 1951.......... 22

    Photograph: Sebastiana (Gianino) Monti 1951.................... 22

    Photograph: Monti Headstone in Sts. Peter and Paul Cemetery.......... 24

    Photographs: 50th Wedding Anniversary Party 1951................. 25

    Photograph: Frank Monti's Wedding Reception 1947................ 26

**4. Monti Siblings Born in St. Louis, Missouri.** . . . . . . . . . . . . . . . . . . . . . . . . . 27

    Document: 1930 United States Census for St. Louis, Missouri . . . . . . . . . . . . 28

    Photograph: Veronica (Vera) Monti 1941. . . . . . . . . . . . . . . . . . . . . . . . . . . 29

    Photograph: Josephine Theresa (Monti) Gianino . . . . . . . . . . . . . . . . . . . . . 32

    Photograph: Maria Margaret (Monti) Viviano-Willis . . . . . . . . . . . . . . . . . . 33

    Photograph: Carmelo Monti. . . . . . . . . . . . . . . . . . . . . . . . . . . . . . . . . . . . 34

    Documents: Newspaper Headlines and Photographs – *St. Louis Globe Democrat* . 35

    Documents: Newspaper Headlines and Photographs – *St. Louis Post-Dispatch* . . . 36

    Photograph: Dominic Joseph Monti. . . . . . . . . . . . . . . . . . . . . . . . . . . . . . . 37

    Photograph: Salvatore Joseph Arturo Monti. . . . . . . . . . . . . . . . . . . . . . . . . 39

    Photograph: Dominica Marie (Monti) Marku . . . . . . . . . . . . . . . . . . . . . . . 40

    Photograph: Flad Avenue House Front Porch in 1943. . . . . . . . . . . . . . . . . . 41

    Photograph: Sebastiano (Charles) Joseph Monti Sr. . . . . . . . . . . . . . . . . . . . 42

    Photograph: Charles Monti with Parents . . . . . . . . . . . . . . . . . . . . . . . . . . 43

    Photograph: Francisco Carmelo Monti. . . . . . . . . . . . . . . . . . . . . . . . . . . . 45

    Photograph: Rosario Guiseppe Monti . . . . . . . . . . . . . . . . . . . . . . . . . . . . 46

    Photograph: Veronica Mary (Monti) Combrevis. . . . . . . . . . . . . . . . . . . . . 47

    Photograph: Monti Family Gathering circa 1955 to 1960 . . . . . . . . . . . . . . . 48

**5. Italian Names: Demographics, Etymology, and Traditions** . . . . . . . . . . . . . . . 49

    Illustration: Trinacria. . . . . . . . . . . . . . . . . . . . . . . . . . . . . . . . . . . . . . . . 51

**6. Descendants of Pietro Gianino.** . . . . . . . . . . . . . . . . . . . . . . . . . . . . . . . . . 53

    Photograph: Three Generations at the 50th Wedding Anniversary Party 1951 . . . 62

**Bibliography.** . . . . . . . . . . . . . . . . . . . . . . . . . . . . . . . . . . . . . . . . . . . . . . . . 63

**Proper Name Index.** . . . . . . . . . . . . . . . . . . . . . . . . . . . . . . . . . . . . . . . . . . 67

**About the Author.** . . . . . . . . . . . . . . . . . . . . . . . . . . . . . . . . . . . . . . . . . . . 75

**Add Your Own Notes** . . . . . . . . . . . . . . . . . . . . . . . . . . . . . . . . . . . . . . . . . 77

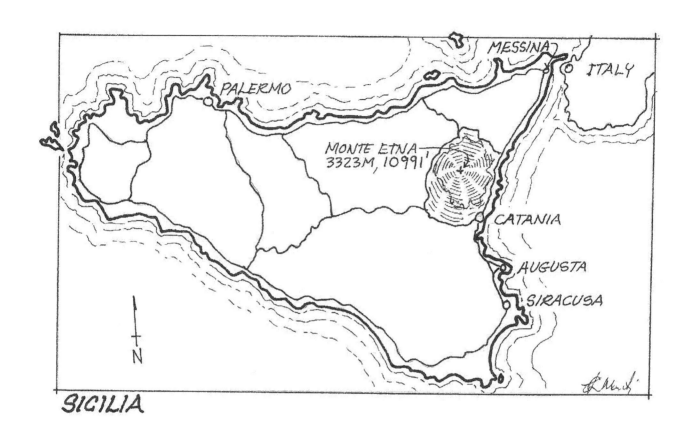

SICILIA

**Map of Sicily**
Illustration courtesy of Carmelo L. Monti AIA

# Introduction

Their generation is dying — those Americans born prior to the Great Depression. Many of them were children of immigrants, the first generation born on American soil, and one by one, their unique stories will disappear into the larger archetype sometimes referred to as the "Greatest Generation" for their endurance and patriotism during the 20th century's good times and bad, unless they are recorded before it's too late.

Research on the family tree for one group of immigrants — the Montis and Gianinos of St. Louis, Missouri — and their children, that first-generation, revealed a complex and interesting picture. It was a richly textured story with exotic city names, an erupting volcano—Monte Etna—and ship's registries that offer both clues and mysteries. There were harrowing voyages across the ocean and entrepreneurial activities of all sorts, including bootlegging during Prohibition. There were sailors, brickyard laborers, foundry workers, and gamblers. Heroics during World War Two. Orphans and children who died in infancy. There was death by St. Louis encephalitis, heart disease, and a shootout with the police.

Their story is mostly urban and recent to the U.S., with four generations or less calling themselves American. Arriving in Boston in the early 1900's then moving west to St. Louis, the earliest Montis and Gianinos maintained their close-knit Sicilian Catholic ethnic identity, and they passed that forward to their children. The eldest daughters entered marriages arranged in the style of the Old World but as time passed, those customs were rejected by the youngest siblings. Their collective stories are a saga decades in the making, a study in the contrasts found in American society — the dichotomy of divergent cultures resolved through matrimony in this big proverbial melting-pot known as the United States.

Their family histories, genealogy, and the pages of this book are loosely derived from an original booklet first produced in 2003 for a small family reunion. For this expanded book-length version I have added new illustrations by Carmelo L. Monti, many more photos from the collections of Sheila Monti-Molina and the Milda (Kaempfe) Monti Estate, and a new chapter that focuses on the early 20th century generation — those Monti siblings born between 1908 and 1928. Each of their stories was produced with help from many cousins, all contributing tidbits of information, detailed stories of their parents' early lives, and anecdotes from their childhoods about their aunts and uncles. Carmelo L. Monti was instrumental in contacting each of them and drawing out the details. Dozens of e-mails and letters were exchanged between them and the author.

Three of those Monti siblings, living at the time of writing in 2009, contributed material for their own biographies. At the time of publication in 2011 only one of that first generation remains with us. Like their siblings and generations before them, they will always be children of Sicily—children of Monte Etna.

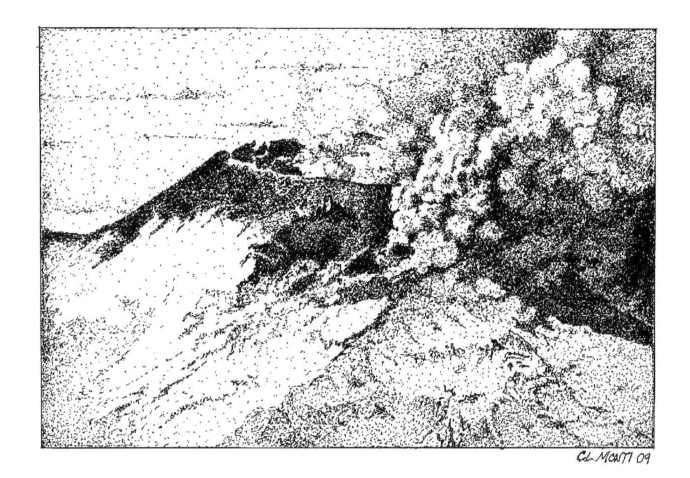

## Monte Etna
### Sicily, Italy
10,991 feet high
The tallest volcano in Europe
A venerable and awesome namesake
Illustration courtesy of Carmelo L. Monti AIA

# Chapter One

## ANCIENT AND EMIGRATION HISTORY OF
## ELIGIO MONTE AND GIANINO FAMILY MEMBERS

At the turn of the century, from 1880 to 1930, four and one-half million Italians immigrated to the United States, among them Eligio Monte (later Monti) and his wife Sebastiana Gianino, and her parents Carmelo Gianino and Santa (Gianino) Gianino. They came from two cities — Monte from Catania in the province of Catania and all three Gianinos from Augusta in Siracusa, on the island of Sicily, which is the largest island in the Mediterranean. For most, their dates and places of birth, marriage and death are known, and there are enough documents to demonstrate that there were many common and shared experiences between them. They also shared the same tumultuous ancient history.

Cave paintings dating to 8000 BC have been found on Sicily, so the island has been inhabited for a very long time. Major groups that colonized it during ancient times included the Phoenicians from Carthage, Greeks, Romans, Vandals, Ostrogoths, Byzantines, and Arabs. The earliest recorded inhabitants of the city of Catania were the Calcidesi in 729 B. C. Every civilization that has conquered Sicily left its architecture, genetic material, and theology. Architectural examples include Sicanian, Greecian, and Roman temples. Mythically, for some, Cyclops lived on Monte Etna; for others, Volcan used the volcano as his forge. In Homer's Odyssey Sicily was named Thrinakie (later Trinacria), meaning "Isle with Triangle's Form." During the two centuries that the Arabs ruled, mosques and Islam became widespread as Sicilian women married the Moorish men and became part of their harems.

The historical traces of synagogues and early Christian churches and catacombs are more difficult to find, and they date from when St. Paul preached to them in violation of Roman law. By the 6th century, Sicily was largely Christianized, with a few small Jewish communities. The first Jews in Sicily were brought as slaves by the Romans before the 1st century AD. By 1492, they made up 5% to 8% of the island's population so when Jews were banished from Spanish territories, rather than leave, many on Sicily converted to Catholicism and romanized their surnames (Ex. Rabbi became Rabbini).

In 1061 the Normans took over the island, tore down all signs of Arab culture, Latinized the island's Christians toward Roman Catholicism, and left their genes for blonde and redheaded Sicilians. Frederick II "the August," a Schwabian king from Hohenstaufen, built castles in Siracusa and Catania in 1220 to 1250. He established the town of Augusta in 1232, building another castle and developing the harbor and trade center. Frederick's successor Manfred was murdered by Charles of Anjou, but the French aristocracy was so hated by the Sicilians that they revolted.

By 1302, the Aragonese (Spanish) took over and held control until 1734. Several events happened during their reign that influenced the future development of both Catania and Augusta. During the war between the French and Spanish in 1676, the town of Augusta was severely damaged and much had to be rebuilt. In 1669, major eruptions of Monte (Mount) Etna devastated the city of Catania. In 1693 an earthquake leveled the city and killed two-thirds of its inhabitants. The Aragonese rebuilt Catania in the Baroque style and many of those buildings still remain. Nearby Augusta was also heavily damaged, and its castle had to be rebuilt.

The Austrians briefly controlled Sicily after defeating the Aragonese, but then the Bourbons of Spain took over. They remained in control until 1861 when the unification of Italy placed Sicily under the Kingdom of Italy. Eligio Monte and all three Gianinos were born as citizens of that Kingdom, between 1865 and 1887. Victor Emmanuel III became the King of Italy in 1900 and he was their king at the time they left Sicily for the United States.

A study of Sicilian history shows that the secret societies called "Mafia" were born on Sicily as a way for the severely impoverished peasants to destroy the fabulously wealthy landowners, who had become established in Roman times. Later, the unification of Italy in 1861 led to further impoverishment because the Kingdom of Italy did not allow industrialization to flow to Sicily and it unfairly taxed them. Eighty per cent of Italians, including Sicilians, were illiterate tenant farmers, farm workers, and day workers. Most owned a house and a small parcel of land. The remaining twenty percent were skilled craftsmen, scholars, or professionals. Only a tiny number were aristocratic. Catania in particular became seriously afflicted with poverty and with crime and violence associated with the Mafia. Mob related gun battles in broad daylight and murders by hit men continue there to this day.

Clearly, the history of Catania was also closely tied to Monte Etna, considering the name derived from *katane*, meaning "flaying knife" or "grater," and it's thought to be a reference to the sharp, prickly lava on which the city was built. At 10,991 feet, it is the tallest volcano in Europe, and it dominates the skyline to the northwest. However, centuries of volcanic eruptions have only killed about seventy-seven people. Fifty-nine of those died in 1843 while they watched the advance of lava and there was a sudden steam explosion. That event would have been in the memory of people living at the time of the birth of Eligio Monte (*sic*) in Catania on February 5, 1877. He probably personally witnessed a series of flank eruptions on Monte Etna that occurred from 1874 to 1892, including two large eruptions when he was ages nine and fourteen.

Oral family history says that Eligio was an orphan, perhaps left in a basket on the Gianino's doorstep, and that his parents are unknown. Family mythology includes the notion that he was fathered by nobility with a mistress who could not keep the child. His birth record, shown on the adjacent page, from Catania lists no parents' names, and that appears to confirm his orphan status but discounts the basket story, given his birth in Catania and their residence twenty-five miles away in Augusta.

A reasonable assumption would be that Eligio saw the Italian Navy as a way out of the many economic and social problems of Catania when he joined in July 1897, at age 20. Not far away, the town Augusta had a Navy base, and he likely went there. Carmelo Gianino, from Augusta, indicated that he also had been a sailor, so it is likely that is how Eligio met his future wife Sebastiana Gianino (Carmelo's daughter). He left the Navy at age 23 on January 10, 1901, and married Sebastiana later that year on December 1, 1901 in Augusta, when he was 24 and she was only 15-years-old. (See the marriage record on page 6.) If Eligio and Sebastiana had children that early in their marriage, there is no known record of them. Their first known child Arturo was born in September or October 1903 in Sicily.

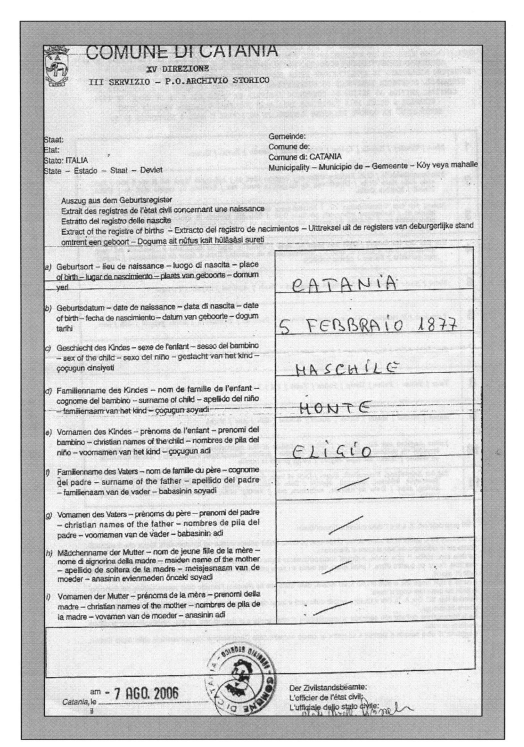

**Birth Record for Eligio Monte**
Image courtesy of Victoria Monti

AUGUSTA
COMUNE

SIRACUSA
PROVINCIA

**UFFICIO DELLO STATO CIVILE**

Estratto per riassunto dai registri degli atti di

# MATRIMONIO

Anno 1901  Parte I^ Serie //  N. 115

Dal registro degli atti di matrimonio di questo Comune, anno - parte - serie e numero sopra indicati, risulta ch

il giorno UNO _____ del mese di DICEMBRE

dell'anno 1901

contrassero matrimonio in AUGUSTA

1) MONTE Eligio
    nato in CATANIA
    DI ANNI VENTIQUATTRO

2) GIANINO Sebastiana
    nato in AUGUSTA
    DI ANNI QUINDICI

ANNOTAZIONI(1): (NESSUNA)==

Per estratto dall'originale, ai sensi degli articoli 106 e seguenti del D.P.R. 3 novembre 2000, n. 396, esente da imp
di bollo ai sensi dell'art. 7, comma 5, della legge 29 dicembre 1990, n. 405.
Il presente estratto ha validità di 6 mesi dalla data di rilascio(2).

(1) Comprese le convenzioni matrimoniali di cui all'art. 162, 2° comma, del Codice Civile e art. 228 legge 19-5-1975, n. 151.
(2) Il presente certificato è ammesso dalle pubbliche amministrazioni nonché dai gestori o esercenti di pubblici servizi anche oltre i termini di validità nel caso in cui l'interessato dichiari, in fondo al documento
informazioni contenute nel certificato stesso non hanno subito variazioni dalla data di rilascio (art. 41 D.P.R. 28 dicembre 2000, n. 445).

data 1 9 LUG 2006

Timbro

IL L'Ufficiale Dello Stato Civile
Dott. Marcello Richera

Il/la sottoscritto/a, ai sensi e per gli effetti dell'art. 41, D.P.
dicembre 2000, n. 445, consapevole delle sanzioni previste in ca
falsa dichiarazione, dichiara che le informazioni contenute nel pre
certificato non hanno subito variazioni dalla data di rilascio.

data _____ firma _____

**Marriage Record for Eligio Monte and Sebastiana Gianino**
Image courtesy of Victoria Monti

**Eligio and Sebastiana (Gianino) Monti**
St. Louis, Missouri circa 1922-1923
Photograph courtesy of Milda (Kaempfe) Monti Estate

**Ellis Island, New York**
Port of Entry for Eligio Monte and the Gianino Family
Photograph from Library of Congress c. 1913

On February 25, 1903, Eligio Monte (*sic*) arrived in New York City at Ellis Island aboard the *SS Equita*. Records show he was 26 years old, a laborer, arriving in the U.S. for the first time and planning to visit his cousin Guiseppe Gianino, on 21st Street in Boston, Massachusetts. Aboard with him and also going to Boston were Guiseppe's brothers Domenico Gianino (age 36) and Pietro Gianino (age 19). Guiseppe Fazio and Carmelo Puolizzi, cousins like Eligio, were also on board and headed for Boston. Only Pietro was single. Even though the record shows the other men as being married, no wives are shown alongside their names. The women were most likely back in their homes in Augusta, Sicily, Italy, waiting, including the then-pregnant Sebastiana.

Eligio eventually returned to Augusta in 1904. His second and final trip to the U.S. was aboard the *SS Sicilian Prince* that arrived at Ellis Island on August 12, 1905. He indicated that he had been in the U.S. before, in Boston in 1903, for an undetermined length of time. This time he said he was a sailor and was going to St. Louis, Missouri, to a relative Sebastiano Gianino on Shaw Avenue, who was perhaps one of the aforementioned Sebastianos, a cousin or uncle or even his wife's brother. In 1904, the City of St. Louis hosted both the World's Fair and the Olympics, and it was the fourth largest and fastest growing city in the U.S. Although Eligio stated in the 1905 ship's registry that he had been in Boston, he surely had heard about the Fair. If his cousins had attended or if they had gone to St. Louis to work during the Fair, he may have learned of job opportunities, and this would explain the change in location from Boston to St. Louis.

Sebastiana Gianino was finally able to join her husband Eligio when she arrived in New York City on October 27, 1905, onboard the *SS Nord America* of the La Veloce Line. The ship's manifest shows seven people traveling from Augusta to St. Louis. Six of those seven were going to 5214 Shaw Avenue. Sebastiana and two-year-old Arturo were together. The remaining four included two sailors, 36-year-old Santo Di Mare and 14-year-old Carmelo Russo. The other two were 26-year-old Maria Di Mare traveling to meet her husband Sebastiano Gianino and their child 5-year-old Lou Sebastiano. Recall that Eligio Monte (*sic*) came to St. Louis to his cousin Sebastiano Gianino on Shaw Avenue in August 1905. It seems obvious that his wife Sebastiana was traveling with a group of related people on her journey to the U.S., including another wife and child, and an older protective male. The women were finally leaving Augusta, no longer waiting at home.

8

In 1913, Sebastiana's parents (Eligio's in-laws) arrived from Augusta, Sicily. Oddly, there are two sets of records for this group of five Gianinos traveling together: Carmelo (age 47), Santa (age 46), Alfio (age 11), Domenica (age 9), and Sebastiano (age 14). They show up on the ship's registry for the *SS Venezia* that arrived at Ellis Island on March 21, 1913, but their names are lined out. This could mean either they boarded ship but were asked to depart before the ship left port, or (hypothetically) they actually arrived in the U.S. but were denied entry and forced to return to Italy. They also show up on the registry for the *SS Santa Anna* that arrived 34 days later on April 25, 1913. Since travel time is about 20 days each way, it appears that they attempted to travel in March but were not permitted to do so; then they succeeded in April. A good guess would be that in March some member of the group was sick with a cold or flu and they were told they could be denied entry into the U.S. In both records, Carmelo indicated that they were traveling to St. Louis, Missouri to his son-in-law Eligio Monte (*sic*) at 5242 Wilson Avenue. Also listed, as a relative remaining in Augusta was Sebastiana Daniele, the mother of Carmelo Gianino.

Carmelo Gianino indicated in April that he had previously been in the U.S. in St. Louis, Missouri, from 1905 to 1911. However, earlier in March on the *Venezia* records, he indicated that he had been in the U.S. from 1908 to 1912. There is no explanation for the discrepancy, but in either case, he had been separated from his wife and children for a very long time, between four and six years.

In searching the Ellis Island records, there are a total of nine male Carmelo Gianinos who arrived in the U.S. One (age 37) arrived on April 8, 1905, aboard the *SS Citta di New York*, along with his son Pietro (age 17). Both are listed as sailors heading to #5 Hale Street in Boston to their cousin Pietro Gianino, possibly the same Pietro who had traveled in 1903 with Eligio. Also aboard the *Citta* were two of the elder Pietro's brothers Domenico (age 36) and Salvatore (age 34); Sebastiano Gianino (age 12) the son of Domenico; and another Sebastiano Gianino (age 16) who had been in Boston 1902-1904. All three of the adults indicated that they had been in the U.S. before. Domenico and Salvatore had been in Boston from 1903 to 1905. Therefore, it's possible that this was the same Domenico Gianino who traveled with Eligio in 1903.

It seems very plausible that Carmelo and his son Pietro first went to Boston to visit cousins and to become established in the U.S. before heading west to St. Louis. Perhaps they waited there from April to August until Eligio arrived so they could all travel together. This would explain Carmelo's assertion in 1913 that he had been in St. Louis from 1905 to 1911, rather than in Boston.

In the records for his 1905 trip, Carmelo said that he had been in Boston for ten months in 1904. Looking back again at the nine listed Carmelo Gianinos, there are three shown as arriving in 1904, but only one was near the correct age. He was a 37-year-old sailor who arrived aboard the *SS Germania* on March 17, 1904, and he was headed to his cousin Domenica Bramanti at 11 Pitts Street in Boston. There are no other connections to this particular name or address. It is possible that Eligio, and perhaps others from that first group of five, had already left Boston and returned to Augusta.

Interestingly, there was another Gianino aboard the *SS Santa Anna* when it arrived in April 1913. It was a 3-month-old baby girl named Santa Gianino traveling with her mother Leonarda De Luca to her father Pietro Gianino at 5143 Wilson Ave. in St. Louis, Missouri. The Pietro to whom they were returning was the son of Carmelo who accompanied him in 1905, first to Boston, then to St. Louis. Pietro likely also returned to Augusta, perhaps in 1911 with Carmelo, where he married Leonarda, started a family, and then returned to St. Louis before the birth of their child Santa, as all the men had done. Note that Leonarda was leaving behind her mother Francesco Passanese, and that earlier in 1908, Domenico Gianino and Sebastiano Passanese had formed a fruit business in Boston.

## Ancestors to the Emigrant Generation

The names for Carmelo and Santa Gianino's parents were found on their Missouri death certificates. Carmelo's death certificate listed both his father (Pietro Gianino) and his mother (Sebastiana Daniele). His mother's name was also found on his Ellis Island ship's registry. Santa's father's name (Dominic Gianino) was shown on her death certificate, but her mother was listed as unknown.

Many people named Gianino have death certificates online at the Missouri Archives website. Some of them offer a few clues to ancestors but little conclusive evidence. For example, Dominico Gianino (b. November 11, 1870 in Italy) lived at 5240 Bischoff, just a few doors down from Carmelo and Santa. He was only four or five years younger than them and was born in Italy the same year as the Domenico Gianino who traveled with Carmelo through Ellis Island in 1905. His death certificate shows his parents were Sebastian Gianino and Conchetta DePetro. There is a good chance he was a first cousin to either or both Carmelo or Santa, that his father Sebastian was a brother to one or both of their fathers, Dominic or Pietro. By piecing together several other death certificates and the 1920 census, this Dominico Gianino was married to Giuseppa (Josephine) Balsamo, and they had numerous children (Sebastiano Charles, Stephen, Joseph and Carmello to name a few) who subsequently had their own families. One son, Sebastiano Charles born in 1893, was probably the 12-year-old Sebastiano who traveled to Boston in 1905 with his father Domenico to his Uncle Pietro, who was a cousin to Carmelo. Therefore, that line of Gianinos is almost certainly related to the line produced by Carmelo and Santa, but the "how" will likely never be known.

In summary, if the records are pieced together correctly, they show that Eligio Monte (*sic*) traveled to the U.S. from Italy on two occasions; that his wife Sebastiana Gianino made one trip and permanently relocated to St. Louis, Missouri, in October 1905; that Carmelo Gianino traveled on three occasions, bringing Santa and three children on his final trip; and that numerous Gianino cousins came and went to Boston and St. Louis, with unknown numbers in both cities, and numerous complicated relationships left undefined.

## The Name Monte became Monti, and the Odd "Munti" Spelling

Census records are notorious for misspelled names, as the quality of the recording was dependent on individual census taker's accuracy; for that reason, genealogy researchers spend hours searching for irregular spellings of names, knowing that they are just that - irregularities. Eligio and Sebastiana appear on the 1910 St. Louis census as Louis (his middle name) and Sebastana Monden (*sic*) in badly mangled, nearly illegible handwriting. On the 1920 St. Louis census their surname was spelled Monti. Robert Willis discovered another odd spelling in the 1930 St. Louis census when the family lived near Downtown on Goode Avenue. In the microfilmed copy of the original 1930 handwritten record, the name is clearly spelled Munti.

Family folklore suggested that the original spelling for Monti might be Munti. One source of this myth stems from sloppy handwriting. Numerous handwritten documents show that when the letter "o" is written casually, especially in cursive style, with the top of the letter not closed, it can be read as a "u" by someone who does not already know the name. The most compelling source for the error is found in three newspaper articles: the June 18, 1933 newspaper articles in both the *St. Louis Post-Dispatch* and *St. Louis Globe Democrat* about the death of Carmelo Munti (*sic*) and a short announcement for the 50th Wedding Anniversary for Mr. and Mrs. Louis Munti (*sic*) in an unknown newspaper in 1951. The 1930 census where the name is clearly spelled Munti contributes to the confusion (see page 28).

Examination of other records shows that older personal records (Eligio's birth record from Catania, marriage record from Augusta, several ships' registries from Ellis Island) all spell the name Monte. The earliest known records of the Monti spelling found to date are the birth record for Maria Monti (b. April 22, 1912) and the 1920 census. Finally, both Eligio and Sebastiana filed Alien Registration Forms with the U.S. government in 1940 and they spelled their name Monti. All of their children, grandchildren, and beyond have spelled their name Monti since birth on official documents.

Etymology of the name is also a factor, and that topic is addressed at length in another chapter. Monte and Monti are both considered Italian in origin, whereas Munte or Mundy is Germanic. The spelling Munti cannot be found in such studies, suggesting that Munti as a name does not really exist. Statistically, Monte and Monti appear with considerable distribution in various places such as census records for the U.S. and Italy. The names Munte or Munti appear only a few times in all U.S. census records, probably in error, and never in Italian records found to date. Mundy does have some small representation in U.S. census records.

Therefore, the logical conclusion is that the name was only misspelled as Munti on a few occasions, albeit public and important ones, by outsiders and was never intentionally changed to or from that spelling by family members. The original surname Monte became Monti as early as 1912 and we will never know why it changed.

**1920 United States Census for St. Louis, Missouri**
One early document with the Monti name spelled with an "i"
Image from microfilm provided by Orange County Library System

**Feast of St. Domenic Parade Along Hale Street**
Boston, Massachusetts circa 1954
Photographs courtesy of the West End Historical Association, Boston MA

# Chapter Two

## THE GIANINO FAMILY IN BOSTON

Eligio Monte (*sic*) and his father-in-law Carmelo Gianino went to Boston, Massachusetts, before they went to St. Louis, Missouri. Various records reveal that Gianino relatives probably still live in the Boston area, but the exact nature of their relationship to the Monti family of St. Louis may never be known.

While in Boston in May 2003, Carmelo L. Monti and his wife, author Mary Miller, visited the Italian District on the north side of Boston. The area still has some older Italians who emigrated from Italy in the early 1900's and their descendants. Lining the streets are numerous Italian restaurants and small grocery stores that specialize in Italian food, much like on the Hill in St. Louis, Missouri. We asked two men — one old, one young — for directions to Hale Street. The old man said he thought he recalled Hale being on the West End, but seemed vague. Curiously, he looked very familiar, with the same Roman nose, short stature, and darker complexion that some Monti family members possess. The younger man was more willing to help but didn't recognize the street name, and none of us understood the West End reference. We described Hale as running between South Margin and Green, so he walked us about three blocks over to North Margin. We explained that we were looking for the street where the Gianinos had lived and described the fruit business that Domenico Gianino started. He immediately recognized the Gianino name and said, "Oh, they're a prominent family here, and very wealthy." That assertion has never been verified.

A review of microfilmed City Directories for Boston for the years 1903 to 1905 show the only Gianino was Gaetano Gianino, a porter for the Terminal Co. with no address given. The Ellis Island website shows that Gaetano arrived in the U.S. for the first time on Sept. 17, 1900, and went to Boston to his uncle Gppe. Filoni at 192 North St. He was a farmer from Augusta, Italy. He appears to have been the first Gianino to immigrate to Boston. Later, in 1906, Gaetano's address is shown as 12 Hale Street.

On February 25, 1903, Eligio Monte (*sic*) arrived in New York at Ellis Island aboard the *SS Equita*. He was 26 years old, a laborer, arriving in the U.S. for the first time and planning to visit his cousin Guiseppe Gianino on 21st Street in Boston. Aboard with him and also going to Boston were Guiseppe's brothers Domenico Gianino (age 36) and Pietro Gianino (age 19). Guiseppe Fazio and Carmelo Puolizzi, cousins like Eligio, were also on board and headed for Boston. The microfilmed City Directories show that the only Monte in Boston was Winfred Monte, an artist, probably unrelated to Eligio.

Carmelo Gianino arrived on April 8, 1905, aboard the *SS Citta di New York* at age 37 along with his son Pietro (age 17). Both were listed as sailors heading to 5 Hale Street in Boston to their cousin Pietro Gianino, possibly the same Pietro who had traveled in 1903 with Eligio. Also aboard the *Citta* were two of the elder Pietro's brothers Domenico (age 36) and Salvatore (age 34). Also, there is a Sebastiano Gianino (age 12) shown as the son of Domenico. Yet another Sebastiano Gianino (age 16) was going to his uncle Pietro. Four of these Gianinos, Carmelo, Domenico, Salvatore, and the 16-year old Sebastiano, indicated that they had been in Boston before.

In 1907, Domenico Gianino also appeared in the Boston City Directory at 21 Hale Street. By 1908, he had a fruit business in partnership with Sebastiano Passanese at 177 W. Broadway. Also in 1908 Francesco Gianino appeared at 34 South Margin. In 1910 "Lena, widow of Guiseppe" appeared at 24 Hale Street, along with Gaetano, Pietro, and Sebastino Gianian. The Gianino-Passanese fruit business was still on Broadway, and Francesco was still on South Margin. (Recall the previously mentioned Leonarda De Luca and her three-month old daughter Santa Gianino, heading to her husband Pietro Gianino in St. Louis, Missouri. Leonarda left behind in Augusta her mother Francesca Passanese.)

In 1942, the Boston City Directory listed twenty-four Gianinos, among them Dominic, Frank, and Natale with his wife Rose, who all lived at 56 Hale Street. Emanuel, Lucy, Pietro, and Sebastiano all resided at 42 Green. Salvatore and his wife Anna lived at 15 Hale.

According to the 1903 Boston City Directory, Hale Street was in the North Station District and went from 38 Green to 20 South Margin. Our visit to Boston in May 2003, revealed that Hale Street, South Margin and Green Street were gone. They were eliminated during the massive demolition of the entire West End neighborhood after World War Two to make way for such projects as the large State Service Center building. Nearby, a large highway overpass, noted for its bright green paint and built in the 1950's, took out more of the old, Italian neighborhood. This overpass was later torn down and replaced with the "Big Dig" tunnel. Much of the land was turned into a city park, with better street access from the south to the north.

This change has already sparked a surge in the value of real estate in the Italian district, and the result has been an explosion of home sales and renovations by developers. The older Italians are afraid of loosing what remains of their neighborhood to wealthier people looking for a home in the city, and there is no doubt that this area will see significant change. In 2003, we found a small 850-square-foot, renovated apartment-style condominium, one of three units in a typical four-story brick row house, for sale for $449,000.

While staying in Boston, Carmelo did additional research at the library, including searching through maps on microfiche and talking to people who have lived in Boston a long time. Finally, a co-worker found a book *Boston's West End* by Anthony Sammarco that describes the demolition of the neighborhood and contains dozens of photos taken before its demise. Two photographs on page 12 show four-story apartment buildings along narrow Hale Street, crowded with Italians in their confirmation finery during a parade down Hale Street and throughout the West End for the Feast of St. Domenic in 1954. These were the same buildings and the same streets where Eligio Monte and the earliest Gianinos in America lived and walked from 1903 to 1905.

## West End Neighborhood
### Boston, Massachusetts

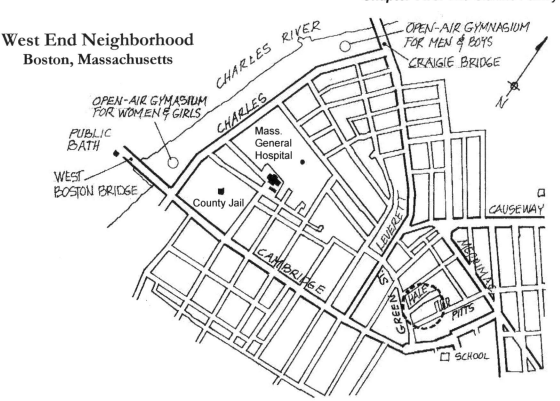

## FROM ONE CITY TO ANOTHER:
### From Boston's West End Neighborhood . . . To . . . The Hill in St. Louis, Missouri

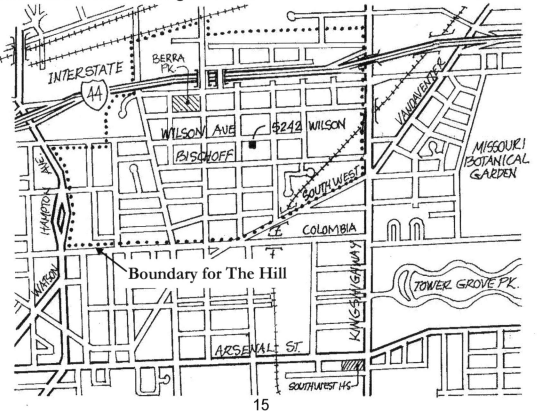

### The Family of Eligio and Sebastiana (Gianino) Monti
St. Louis, Missouri
circa late 1930s

**Standing Left to Right:** Sebastiano (Charles), Dominic (Don), Joseph (Joe), Eligio, Salvatore (Sam), Francesco (Frank), and Rosario (Roy)
**Seated Left to Right:** Dominica (Babe), Maria (Mary), Sebastiana, Josephine (Josie), and Veronica (Vera)

Photograph courtesy of Milda (Kaempfe) Monti Estate

# Chapter Three

## POST-EMIGRATION HISTORY IN
## St. LOUIS, MISSOURI

As mentioned in their emigration history, Eligio Monte (*sic*) married Sebastiana Gianino in Augusta, Sicily, on December 1, 1901, when he was 24 years old and she was only 15. If Eligio and Sebastiana had children very early in their marriage, there is no known record of them. Their first known child Arturo was born in September or October 1903. Eligio made two trips to the U.S. in 1903 and 1905, and Sebastiana and Arturo finally joined her husband in St. Louis, Missouri, in October 1905.

**Santa (Gianino) Gianino**
(1866-1955)
1951 Monti Anniversary Party

The 1910 United States census for St. Louis, Missouri includes Louis (his middle name) and Sebastana Monden (*sic*) living with three other families at 5320 Shaw Avenue. The census shows that Louis was 34 and worked as a laborer in a brickyard. Sebastana (*sic*) was 24 and had borne two children, but only one was alive. Oddly, that child (probably Joseph born in 1908) was not shown on the census, and the deceased child was probably Arturo. (This confirms that Sebastiana bore only one child in Sicily — Arturo — and he emigrated with her.) They had been married for five years, had emigrated in 1905, and were both aliens born in Italy, as were their parents.

In 1913, Sebastiana's parents Carmelo and Santa (Gianino) Gianino and three of her siblings (Alfio, Domenica, and Sebastiano) arrived from Augusta at her home at 5242 Wilson Avenue. By the 1920 St. Louis census, these families had changed locations again but were living in close proximity on The Hill, a traditional Italian district in southwest St. Louis. Carmelo was 55 and worked as a laborer in a brickyard. Santa was 50 and worked as a homemaker. Their home at 5224 Bischoff Avenue was rented. They were both still aliens, spoke no English, and neither one could read or write. A 26-year-old son Samuel (probably Sebastiano) had been naturalized as a citizen in 1919, spoke English and worked as a moulder in an iron foundry. A 16-year-old daughter Minni (probably Domenica) was also a naturalized citizen and spoke English.

**Carmelo and Santa (Gianino) Gianino**
(1865-1920)        (1866-1955)
Photograph of image on the headstone courtesy of Katie from Findagrave.com

Not long after that 1920 census was taken, Carmelo Gianino died on April 13, 1920, of St. Louis encephalitis, a mosquito-borne viral infection, after being sick for ten days. His Missouri death certificate shows his industry as a laborer in the Christy Clay Co and his father as Pietro Gianino and mother as Sebastiana Daniele. He was buried in Sec. 38, Lot 2091 in Sts. Peter and Paul Cemetery at age 54 on April 19, 1920.

On page 19, a photograph of the couple's headstone demonstrates some of the difficulties in documenting facts by genealogical researchers. While Carmelo's Missouri death certificate shows his birthday to be November 24, 1865, this headstone shows it to be "DIC" (December in Italian) 15, 1866. His first name is misspelled "Camelo" on the headstone (as is Santa's — "Sanda"). His date of death on April 13, 1920 is the same in both places. On Santa's Missouri death certificate, her birthday is shown as October 5, 1875, but on this headstone it's "OTT" (October in Italian) 5, 1870, which agrees with her declaration of being aged 50 on the 1920 St. Louis census. However, she also said in March 1913 that she was 46, placing her birth year in 1866.

**Headstone for Carmelo and Santa (Gianino) Gianino**
Sts. Peter and Paul Cemetery, St. Louis, Missouri
Photograph of headstone courtesy of Katie from Findagrave.com

In the 1920 census (see page 11), Eligio and his wife Sebastiana Monti (*sic*) were living in the house they owned with a mortgage at 5242 Wilson. They were both still aliens and said they could read and write (probably Italian) and could speak English. He was an ironworker at a foundry and she was a homemaker. They had seven children, aged 9 months to 11 years, all born in Missouri. A roomer named Dominik Franco (perhaps Di Franco), aged 53, lived with them, and he worked as a laborer at the clay pipe company.

Bischoff and Wilson streets are just one block apart on The Hill in St. Louis. A visit there in February 2003, showed that the Wilson Avenue house was still standing. Eligio's son Charles Monti Sr. recalled that his father dug out the basement floor to build a still during the 1920's and later put a second still in the brick garage in the back yard.

**An Early Monti Residence**
5242 Wilson Avenue in St. Louis
Most of the Monti siblings noted in Chapter Four were born in this house with the assistance of midwives.
Photograph courtesy of Mary Miller and Carmelo L. Monti

## Immigration Records

In March 2003, requests were submitted under the Freedom of Information Act, to the U.S. Department of Justice Immigration and Naturalization Service for all immigration records for five people: Eligio Monti, Sebastiana (Gianino) Monti, Alfio Gianino, Santa Gianino, and Sebastiano C. Gianino. In June 2003 records for Eligio, Sebastiana, and Alfio were received. In late 2004 a 26-page file for Sebastiano C. Gianino was received, he was determined to be a distant cousin, and the file was mailed in 2007 to Sharon Egler, who was researching the Gianino family at the time.

## Eligio Monti

Eligio Monti's records consist solely of the Alien Registration Form. He does not appear on the Social Security Death Index website, and therefore likely never became a U.S. citizen.

On September 19, 1940, he filled out the Alien Registration Form required by the U.S. government for all non-citizens. He showed his birthday as February 5, 1877, place of birth as Catania, Catania, Italy and citizenship of Italy. He said he was also known by the name Louis Monti. (His wife called herself Mrs. Luigi Monti on her Form.) He said he was 5'-3" tall, weighed 216 pounds, and had white hair and brown eyes. He lived at 4131 Flad Avenue in St. Louis, Missouri. He first arrived in New York on February 24, 1901, but last arrived on August 12, 1905 on board the *SS Sicilian Prince* of the Prince Line. He said he planned to live in the U.S. permanently, had once applied for citizenship on January 28, 1911, but had never petitioned for naturalization. He was a laborer by occupation but had

Best "Reproducible" Copy Available

Form AR-4
OFFICE USE

1984556

UNITED STATES DEPARTMENT OF JUSTICE
IMMIGRATION AND NATURALIZATION SERVICE

ALIEN REGISTRATION FORM

OFFICE USE

1. (a) My name is ...... Eligio ........ Monti
2. (b) I entered the United States under the name of ...... Eligio Monti
3. (c) I have also been known by the following names ...... Louis Monti
(include maiden name if a married woman, professional names, nicknames, and aliases):

2. (a) I live at ...... 4131 Flad Ave. ...... St. Louis ...... Missouri
(b) My post-office address is ...... Same

3. (a) I was born on ...... February ...... 5 ...... 1877
(b) I was born in (or near) ...... Catania ...... Catania ...... Italy

4. I am a citizen or subject of ...... None, last a citizen of Italy

5. (a) I am a (check one): Male [X] Female [ ]   (b) My marital status is (check one): Single [ ] Married [X] Widowed [ ] Divorced [ ]
(c) My race is (check one): White [X] Negro [ ] Japanese [ ] Chinese [ ] Other ......

6. I am 5 feet, 3 inches in height, weigh 216 pounds, have white hair and brown eyes.

7. (a) I last arrived in the United States at ...... New York ...... on ...... August 12, 1905
(b) I came in by ...... S.S. Sicilian Prince ...... Prince Line
(c) I came as a (check one): Passenger [X] Crew member [ ] Stowaway [ ] Other ......
(d) I entered the United States as a (check one): Permanent resident [X] Visitor [ ] Student [ ] Treaty merchant [ ] Seaman [ ] Official of a foreign government [ ] Employee of a foreign government official [ ] Other ......
(e) I first arrived in the United States on ...... February ...... 24 ...... 1901

8. (a) I have lived in the United States a total of ...... 35 ...... years.
(b) I expect to remain in the United States ...... permanently

9. (a) My usual occupation is ...... Laborer ...... (b) My present occupation is ...... none
(c) My employer (or registering parent or guardian) is ...... none
whose address is ......
and whose business is ......

**Alien Registration Form for Eligio Monti**
September 19, 1940
Document courtesy of U.S. Department of Justice Immigration and Naturalization Service

**Eligio Luigi Monte
a.k.a. Eligio Louis Monti**
(1877-1951)
1951 50th Anniversary Party

no employer. He had served in the Italian Navy from July 15, 1897 to January 10, 1901. Living in the U.S. with him were no parents, but he did have a wife and ten children. He had been arrested and convicted twice for violation of the Volstead Act (Prohibition) in St. Louis, Missouri, in November 1926 (served 2 months in St. Charles, Missouri) and in June, 1932 (served 1 month in Montgomery, Missouri). He listed two club memberships, Regara Augusta Society member since 1913, and the Palma Augusta Protective Club member since 1936.

Note that "Feb. 24, 1901," the "first arrival" date listed on the Form, does not agree with February 25, 1903, shown on Ellis Island records. Because the ship's registry clearly asks "whether ever before in the United States" and his reply was "No," the 1901 date recorded later in 1940 on the Form is likely a typo or error of memory. Bear in mind that Eligio left the Navy on January 10, 1901, and married on December 1, 1901. It seems unlikely that he left the Navy, rushed over to the U.S. and then returned to Sicily by December to marry. Therefore, the correct "first arrived" date most likely was February 25, 1903, making the year 2003 the centennial celebration of the Monti family's first arrival on U.S. soil.

## Sebastiana (Gianino) Monti

Sebastiana Monti's records also consist solely of the Alien Registration Form. She does not appear on the Social Security Death Index website, and therefore likely never became a U.S. citizen.

On October 30, 1940, Sebastiana Monti filled out the Alien Registration Form required by the U.S. government for all non-citizens. She showed her birthday as September 25, 1886, place of birth as Augusta, Siracusa, Italy, maiden name of Gianino and citizenship of Italy. She said she is also known as Mrs. Luigi Monti. She said she was 5'-0" tall, weighed 140 pounds, and had brown hair and gray eyes. She lived at 4131 Flad Ave. in St. Louis, Missouri. She first arrived in New York on October 27, 1905, on board the *SS Nord America* from the La Veloce Line. She said she planned to live in the U.S. permanently, but had never applied for citizenship. She was a housewife by occupation. Living in the U.S. with her were one parent, a husband and ten children. She had been arrested, but never convicted, twice for violation of the Volstead Act (Prohibition) in St. Louis, Missouri, on August 4, 1928 and on December 23, 1932. She listed one club membership in the Palma Augusta mutual aid benefit society, member since 1936.

**Sebastiana (Gianino) Monti**
(1886-1966)
1951 50th Anniversary Party

Note that her birthday of September 25, 1886 shown on the Alien Registration Form, conflicts with September 29, 1887 shown on her death certificate, as recorded by her daughter Mrs. L. Combevis in 1966. Two handwritten family records show her birthday as September 29, 1886. Other sources of her birthday include a 1920 census in which she stated she was 34 years old on her last birthday in 1919, which would place her birth year at 1885. In that same census, she stated that her year of immigration was 1905. Therefore, consider the birthday September 25, 1886, and immigration dates, which she herself verbally provided and swore was true on the Alien Registration Form, the most likely to be correct.

## Ralph (formerly Alfio) Gianino

Alfio Gianino's immigration records are quite complex and consist of numerous documents. Alfio was Sebastiana's brother, and he arrived in the U.S. on April 25, 1913 as a child with their parents Santa and Carmelo Gianino.

On March 8, 1935, Alfio filled out a Declaration of Intention form in St. Louis, Missouri. He resided at 1935 Cooper Street and worked at plastering. He described himself as male, white, dark complexion, blue eyes, brown hair, 5-feet 7-inches tall, weight 145 pounds, Italian nationality, born in Augusta, Italy, on April 20, 1901. He married Carolina on August 17, 1928 and gave her birthday and their children with their birth dates. He arrived in New York aboard the *SS Santa Anna* on April 25, 1913.

On July 23, 1937, Alfio filled out a Petition for Naturalization form in St. Louis, Missouri. He lived at 1935 Cooper Street and worked as a plastering contractor. He stated that he was born on April 20, 1901 in Augusta, Italy. His wife's name was Carolina and they were married on August 17, 1928, in St. Charles, Missouri. He listed her birthday and their children with their birth dates. He arrived in New York aboard the *SS Santa Anna* on April 25, 1913. He renounced allegiance to Victor Emmanuel III, King of Italy. He asked for a legal name change from Alfio to Ralph at the time of naturalization.

His name was changed by decree of court at the time of naturalization from Alfio to Ralph. His Certificate of Citizenship was issued on November 5, 1937. The certificate has a photo of him with a minimal physical description. Later he received Social Security Number 499-01-5819, as shown on the Social Security Death Index website.

## The Later Years

On December 1, 1951, Eligio and Sebastiana Monti celebrated their 50th wedding anniversary.

The matriarch of the family Santa Gianino was at the wedding anniversary party in 1951. She died four years later on December 23, 1955 at the home of Pete Gianino (probably her son Pietro) at 5333 Shaw from acute cardiac failure and "hydrodolic" pneumonia. She was buried in Section 38, Lot 2091 in Sts. Peter and Paul Cemetery at about age 80 on December 28, 1955. There is a big variation between birth years shown on various documents, including 1875 on her death certificate; 1869 on the 1920 census; and 1866 on Ellis Island records. Because her daughter Sebastiana was born in 1886, her birth year was most likely between 1866 and 1869. Consider the Ellis Island record at 1866 to be correct because it was the earliest recorded, and Santa herself provided the information.

Eligio Louis Monti died at age 74 on December 24, 1951 of arteriosclerosis and chronic myocarditis. He was at home, at 4131 Flad Avenue, sitting at the kitchen table when he said, "I am going to bed now and die," which is what he did. His parents remained unknown. Sebastiana (Gianino) Monti died at age 80 on November 13, 1966 from the same type of artery and heart problems, and she is buried next to Eligio in Section 40, Lot 2457. Their headstone includes a memorial to Little Frankie who died as a toddler, and he is buried in Sts. Peter and Paul Cemetery as well.

**Monti Headstone Located in Sts. Peter and Paul Cemetery**
St. Louis, Missouri
Eligio 1877-1951 Father
Sebastiana 1887-1966 Mother
Frank 1922-1924
The original angel was much larger but was stolen, so this smaller replacement was selected to avoid a repeat theft.
Photograph courtesy of Mary Miller and Carmelo L. Monti

### 50th Wedding Anniversary Party for Eligio and Sebastiana Monti
December 1, 1951

**Seated Left to Right:** Santa Gianino, Eligio Monti, and Sebastiana (Gianino) Monti
**Standing Left to Right:** Francisco (Frank), Maria (Mary), Rosario (Roy), Josephine (Josie), Salvatore (Sam), Dominica Marie (Babe), Joseph (Joe), Veronica (Vera), Sebastiano (Charles or Charlie), and Dominic (Don)

Photographs courtesy of Milda (Kaempfe) Monti Estate

**Frank Monti's Wedding Reception July 5, 1947**
**Standing Left to Right:** Sam, Mary, Josie, Babe, Charlie, and Roy Monti
**Seated Left to Right:** Sebastiana, Eligio, Vera, and Frank Monti
Two missing siblings were Don and Joe
Photograph courtesy of Milda (Kaempfe) Monti Estate

# Chapter Four

## MONTI SIBLINGS BORN IN ST. LOUIS, MISSOURI

### Growing Up On The Hill And Beyond

In 1904, St. Louis was a shining beacon of growth and advanced thinking. The World's Fair and Olympics put the city at the center of everyone's attention and no doubt caught the eye of many newly arrived immigrants. With its Palace of Electricity where new inventions like toasters, telephones, and vacuum sweepers awed folks who still used kerosene lamps at home, the Fair was the topic of conversation for years to come.

Eligio Monte (*sic*) was in Boston from 1903 to 1904, so he almost certainly heard stories about the events. Some of his many Gianino cousins probably attended, by taking a steam engine halfway across the continent, and then decided to stay. Eligo returned to Augusta, Sicily in 1904, and when he came back to the U.S. in August 1905 he headed straight to St. Louis, to his cousin Sebastiano Gianino on Shaw Avenue in the heart of The Hill, located near the highest point in the city. His bride Sebastiana (often called Anna) Gianino came later that year in October, bringing with her their first-born son, Arturo.

Clay was discovered in the area around 1830; by 1853 a group of Frenchmen built a socialist commune there; and by the 1890s, Italians were filling up all available shanties and frame tenements as they came to work in the clay pits or to make bricks. By 1904, subdivisions full of homes made with their very own bricks were springing up to meet the demand for better housing as Italian women followed their husbands to the U.S.

A German congregation established the Roman Catholic Church on The Hill in 1892, and by 1900 a small group of Italian parishioners attended services. In 1903, an Italian mission successfully raised funds for their own building; a frame structure for St. Ambrose Church was erected at Marconi and Wilson Avenues; and by 1906 the two-room Parochial School was built. Shaw Elementary School on Columbia opened in 1907. In 1921 the frame church burned, and the Monti family probably watched the fire, as they lived just one block away. By 1926 a new brick and terracotta Lombard Romanesque style church took its place as the social and spiritual center for this burgeoning urban neighborhood. Columbia Theater opened in 1925.

Children filled the streets heading to school, while parents went to work at the brick or clay products factories, or opened their own grocery stores, barber shops and shoe repair services. In 1914 the Ravarino-Freschi Spaghetti and the Blue Ridge Bottling companies became big new employers in the neighborhood. Monti and Gianino women went to work making spaghetti. Eligio Monti, shown as Louis Monden on the 1910 census, worked in a brickyard, but by 1920 he worked at a nearby iron foundry.

Prohibition led the Italians to make their own brew, including Eligio, who had a still in his basement and another in the brick garage at 5242 Wilson Avenue. As grandson Louis C. Monti pointed out, "bootlegging" was a profitable enterprise and gave many immigrants the opportunity to support their families and climb the economic ladder into middle class. Both Eligio and Sebastiana were arrested more than once for it and in 1926 Eligio spent time in jail. Sometime around 1928 or 1929, they left the Wilson Avenue house and rented it to their oldest daughter Josephine and her new husband Santo Gianino. Eligio probably continued to brew his "moonshine" there.

By 1930 they were living northwest of Downtown St. Louis at 2427 Goode Avenue (later renamed Annie Malone Drive) across from the future Homer G. Phillips Hospital (a hospital for blacks-only that opened in 1932) in the Elleardsville (now The Ville) neighborhood, bounded by St. Louis Avenue and Easton (later renamed Martin Luther King), between Taylor Avenue and Sarah Street. The area had grown from 8% African-American in 1920 to 86% by 1930 because it was one of the few areas in city where blacks could own property. Annie Malone, one of the richest black women in American history, lived there.

Two of Eligio's neighbors Henry and Martha Berry, who lived at 2520 Goode, had four children, including a three-year-old son in 1930 named Charles Edward Anderson Berry. Later in life, he was famously known as the rock-n-roll king Chuck Berry. His 1958 hit tune Johnnie B. Goode, once ranked as the 7th greatest rock song of all time by *Rolling Stone Magazine*, memorialized the street name. His original lyrics referred to Johnnie Johnson, his piano player, as a "colored boy" but they were revised to read "country boy" so the song could be played on the radio. Charles Monti recalled having known him.

**1930 United States Census for St. Louis, Missouri**
Image from microfilm provided by Orange County Library System

The 1930 United States Census for St. Louis, Missouri (shown on page 28) recorded Eligio as a "merchant" who ran a "grocery store," a family-run confectionery on the first floor of the flat that they owned, right next door to the then-new Antioch Baptist Church. Imagine for a moment that a little kid named Chuck Berry visited the confectionery to buy penny candy on his way home from church, where his father was a Deacon, then held his mother's hand as they crossed Goode Avenue to walk just one block home.

From under the counter, Eligio was selling booze, this time to his black neighbors who had moved north from Mississippi, Arkansas, and Alabama seeking opportunity and who worked at a wide variety of jobs, such as doctor, carpenter, janitor, chauffeur, or teacher. By 1932, Eligio was arrested for violating the Volstead Act again and served more time in jail. In June 1933, one son Carmelo was shot and killed in a shootout with two Irish policemen on their doorstep, and Eligio was seriously wounded during that incident. It's not hard to imagine seven-year-old Chuck Berry playing stick-ball in the street that Saturday afternoon, hearing the gunshots and ambulance sirens, and running down the block to see the commotion. It was a day the Monti siblings never forgot.

Today, both the Monti confectionery and the Berry house are gone. Antioch Baptist Church acquired the decayed buildings or empty lots on the entire adjacent block and expanded, more than doubling the size of their facility. The block where the Berry house stood is now part of the enormous, much-expanded Homer G. Phillips Hospital complex.

Nearby, Kerry Patch was a tough, Irish immigrant neighborhood also to the north of Downtown, sitting between Biddle and Mullanphy Streets, from 9th Street to Jefferson Avenue. Irish gangs ruled the streets and periodically outside gangs entered its boundaries to create mayhem. Much of this had to do with turf wars over the illegal sale of alcohol. Charlie Monti Sr. admitted that on a few occasions he and his brothers participated in fights between the Irish and the Italians, but he did not elaborate other than to say, "Sometimes we showed them they weren't so tough." Furthermore, many Irish went to work for the police and fire department, jobs considered beneath the dignity of the established St. Louis citizenry.

Repeal of Prohibition in December 1933 brought a flush of new taverns, nightclubs, and restaurants to the area along Southwest and Marconi Avenues on The Hill. By 1940 the Monti family had moved again, this time to the Shaw neighborhood at 4131 Flad Avenue and closer to their old, Italian neighbors. Sam and Josie (Monti) Gianino are thought to have been the owners of that large two-

**Veronica (Vera) Monti – 1941**
4131 Flad Avenue
Notice the banner in the window with five stars representing five boys serving in World War Two: Don, Sam, Charlie, Frank and Roy.

Photograph courtesy of Veronica Combrevis

29

story stone and brick house. By then, Eligio and Anna belonged to at least two ethnic, Sicilian "protective" or "mutual aid" societies, the Palma Augusta and the Regara Augusta.

In these active, bustling environments, Eligio and Sebastiana parented fifteen named children. Assumed first-born son Arturo arrived with his mother from Sicily in 1905 then disappeared from records. Oral family history indicates that two daughters, Theresa and Katherine, died in infancy, but no records have been found. Little Frankie died at age two in 1924. Only eleven survived to adulthood.

While some family members place the number of children at sixteen, seventeen, or even eighteen, no documentation has been found to substantiate that assertion. Others have long speculated that Eligio and Sebastiana left children behind in Sicily to explain the higher number. Doing the math, the reason for such speculation becomes clear. Eligio married Sebastiana on December 1, 1901. In theory a first child might have arrived around September or October 1902, with Sebastiana pregnant a second time when Eligio left Sicily for the first time around January 1903. Arturo was born in September or October 1903 in Sicily during Eligio's absence. He returned to Sicily for a while in 1904, so Sebastiana could have conceived a third time during that period, with a child born anytime during early to mid-1905. Eligio left Sicily again around June 1905. By October 1905, Arturo was two years old when arriving at Ellis Island with his mother. It all adds up. In theory Sebastiana could have conceived two other children, but why would she bring a two-year-old to the U.S. and leave behind a three-year-old or a newborn infant? If she left children behind, they were probably stillborn or died as babies, and those two undocumented children could explain why some family members insist that Sebastiana bore as many as eighteen children – not just the fifteen named ones.

However the 1910 St. Louis census throws another kink into all this speculation. On that document Sebastiana said that she had borne two children and only one remained alive. The deceased child was probably Arturo, and, oddly, the living child was not named, but in all likelihood he would have been Joseph, born in 1908. Her assertion in 1910 that she had borne only two children certainly discounts any speculation that she had other children in Italy before emigrating; however if Eligio provided the information to the census taker, perhaps he had forgotten about stillborn babies that he never saw because he was in the U.S. when they were born.

Furthermore, if living children were left behind, a much better guess would be that they were Sebastiana's siblings (not her children)—that her forty-seven-year-old parents Carmelo and Santa Gianino might have left adult children behind when they came to the U.S. in 1913, perhaps daughters in their twenties who were married to husbands who did not want to emigrate.

In conversations with many family members over the years, most have stated that Eligio was a happy, jovial man who earned everyone's respect with his calm, soothing manner; but he had a tough, authoritarian side, too, and he liked to gamble. Sebastiana was his polar opposite. She seldom smiled and was known for delivering tirades in high-pitched, staccato Sicilian with such ferocity that even forty years later the memory brought hurtful looks to the faces of her children as they recalled their youth. She mellowed in old age and delighted in her grandchildren who numbered in the dozens.

Born over a twenty-year span between 1908 and 1928, each of the eleven surviving Monti siblings was born on The Hill, but many grew up in The Ville, and a few of the youngest called what is now the Shaw neighborhood home; most of them spent the majority of their lives in the region; and each one had a unique personality and life experience. Many of the siblings grew up to have passionate personalities with short tempers, held intense opinions, and expressed them with language that would make a sailor blush. Despite their limited educational opportunities they strove for success in their jobs or owned businesses. Most continued to identify themselves as Catholic throughout life, but not all adhered to the dogma or attended mass regularly.

Louis C. Monti wrote, "One of the most important things to remember about the Monti clan is that they lived between two cultures. The brothers and sisters learned and spoke Italian before English. They, in a sense, were caught between two belief systems. One was the superstitious and suspicious of the Old World and the other, the prejudice and hypocrisy of the New World. Only the black man was lower on the caste than the Sicilian at the time. Therefore they elevated themselves by their own prejudice." Those sensibilities and attitudes remained with many of them for their lifetimes.

Although they had many good times together, most also shared a strong sense of envy and extreme competition, which resulted in many arguments, with various factions taking sides. Several of them told their own children that they believed their brothers or sisters really disliked them. After the death of Eligio in 1951, the disagreements sometimes escalated to the point that nobody spoke to each other for weeks, even months on end, but invariably, they would kiss and make-up over a bowl of Sebastiana's "peace-making" Sicilian bean and macaroni soup, then resume their familiar, jovial socializing with family picnics in the park, holiday feasts, anniversary parties, regular card games, gambling on horse races at Cahokia Downs or Fairmount Park in Illinois, and occasional trips to Las Vegas. Life was never dull and they were always drawn back to one another.

Here is a brief glimpse at their lives, told in chronological order of their birth.

## Portraits of the Siblings

### Arturo Gianino Monti (about 1903 - before 1910)

Arturo was probably the first-born son for Eligio and Sebastiana. The only documentation known to exist for him is the ship's registry for the *SS Nord America*. Nineteen-year-old Sebastiana Gianino and her two-year-old son Arturo Gianino were traveling from Augusta, Italy, to the U.S. for the first time, headed to her "husband Monti, Luigi" at 5214 Shaw Ave. in St. Louis, Missouri. She could not read or write. Her husband paid her passage. Arturo's name is below hers. Above his inscribed name, barely visible, is the word "Monti." The word "father" is barely visible on that line along with "ditto" marks under Sebastiana's entries. His father paid his passage. In the 1910 St. Louis census Sebastiana reported that she had borne two children but only one remained alive. Eligio and Sebastiana appeared with numerous children on the 1920 census but Arturo was not included. On her 1940 Alien Registration Form, Sebastiana stated that she had ten children living in the U.S., and they are all accounted for, so he certainly was not living at that time. Frank Monti said that he recalled stories of a younger brother drowning in a creek off of Macklind Avenue, and Sheila Monti-Molina recalled a story of a baby drowning in a bathtub. Perhaps one of those stories involved Arturo. In any case, he probably died before 1910, before the state of Missouri began requiring death certificates, but exactly when or where he is buried will likely never be known.

### Joseph Louis Monti (September 14, 1908 - May 22, 1998)

Joe was probably born at 5320 Shaw Avenue, where his parents were renting at the time of the 1910 St. Louis census, although, oddly, the census taker failed to list his name. In 1920 he appeared as an eleven-year-old living with them at 5242 Wilson Avenue. By the 1930 census, he was a young man at age twenty-two and had moved away from home, but his own household cannot be found on that census. He probably married Theresa Genoni around 1927, and they had two children. At the time of their deaths, they both donated their bodies to St. Louis University for medical research. His son Louis died in 1989, but Joe left behind one daughter and five grandchildren.

## Josephine Theresa (Monti) Gianino (July 4, 1910 – June, 1996)

Josie was the oldest girl and she acquired her nickname quite young, appearing as such in the 1920 St. Louis census while she was still nine years old. She left school after the eighth grade and went to work doing various things — laundry and factory work — to help the family. Around 1928, when her younger sister Mary was forced to reject a suitor because Josie had not yet married, her parents arranged a marriage for her, Sicilian style in the way of the Old World, to Santo Gianino, a distant, much-older cousin. The 1930 St. Louis census shows Santo (age 28) who worked as a laborer in a brickyard, his wife Josephine (age 20), and their one-year-old son Sam, living in a rented house at 5242 Wilson Avenue, which was probably still owned by Josie's father Eligio Monti. Josie had been born and raised there until her family moved up north to Goode Avenue around 1928 or 1929. The couple had been married two years at the time of that census.

During the early 1930s Josie was a precinct captain while active in the Democratic Party. She and Santo are thought to have owned a two-story stone and brick house at 4131 Flad Avenue, where Josie's parents were living in 1940 when they filed their Alien Registration forms. The couple owned taverns in north St. Louis, operating as many as three during the 1940s. After selling them, they "bought a very nice bar on Pine Street in Downtown St. Louis," wrote her son Sam Gianino. "It was eventually bought out by (the) City to make way for the Mansion House Apartments. She sure had a very business (like) mind for an 8th grade grad."

The marriage ended in divorce in 1952, but Josie remained amicable with Santo while she raised their son Sam in the family home on Flad Avenue. Her nephew Louis C. Monti wrote that he, his widowed father Dominic, and his younger brother Don also lived there, sometimes upstairs with "Aunt Jay" who helped to raise the two children, and sometimes downstairs with "Grandma" Sebastiana and Aunt Vera, "depending on who was fighting with who at the time," until the house was sold in 1958. Louis wrote that his Aunt Jay was "a very intuitive person and like Aunt Babe, would have probably been considered 'gifted' in the Old World." Although she was a member of St. Ambrose Church, Louis wrote, "I don't recall her ever being active in the church but she said prayers every night."

Josie worked in a laundry and a drycleaners or as a waitress most of her life, but she also bought an apartment building on Chippewa Street in South St. Louis and lived in one of them for many years. She never learned to drive a car, never drank or smoked, and cooked fabulous homemade ravioli. Later in life, she was known to keep company with a detective friend for companionship. She worked hard to save enough money to purchase two four-plex apartment buildings, in Lakeshire off Old Tesson Ferry Road (Highway 21) in St. Louis County, which she managed until her death from colon cancer in 1996 at age eighty-five, a month shy of her eighty-sixth birthday. She is buried in Resurrection Cemetery, St. Louis, Missouri next to Santo Gianino, who lived his last years with their son Sam and six grandchildren until his death in 1974.

## Maria Margaret (Monti) Viviano-Willis (April 22, 1912 – April 16, 1997)

In April 1912 when Mary was born, her parents Eligio (age 35) and Sebastiana (age 25) were already living at 5242 Wilson Avenue on The Hill. She was baptized at the wood-frame St. Ambrose Church just one block away and her godparents were Anthony and Rosalia Viviano. By the eighth grade, she dropped out of school and went to work. Her brother Charlie said, "Mary gave up her life to help Momma and Papa; she worked hard so the rest of us could finish school and not do without." In the 1930 St. Louis census, at age eighteen, she lived with her parents at 2427 Goode but was working as a "shotter" in a "cleaning place."

Her difficult early life continued when a suitor asked her to marry and she was forced to reject him because her older sister Josie was still single. In two Sicilian style arrangements, Josie married her cousin Santo Gianino, and Mary married Anthony Viviano Jr. in 1931. They had one daughter Kathleen, but soon Mary asked for a divorce. The Viviano family wanted her dead until she proved to Anthony Sr. that his son was beating her, so he gave her his blessing, beat Anthony Jr., and disowned him. She divorced Anthony in 1935 and later married Richard Lee Willis, Jr. around 1942. They had one son, Richard III. While Richard was stationed in Germany with the Army, he became acquainted with a German girl and wanted to bring her back to the U.S. Although Mary loved Richard deeply, they were divorced around 1954, and she never remarried. Richard married the German girl and they remained a couple until his death in 2009.

Mary enjoyed her children and her siblings with their big extended families and she found her happiness with them. She was known to be a good cook with a lasagna recipe that everyone loved. Mary was loud with a boisterous personality, was as competitive as her brothers, and preferred to play card games with them, rather than with the women. When her sister Babe was around, both of them joined the men's game and had a rowdy good time. Mary drove a 1953 Chevrolet Belair. One day her son Ricky, his friends, and a few cousins took it out driving and wrecked the front end. In fear of the "Bucalata" (as she was sometimes called), they stayed up all night repairing and painting the car, finishing just as Mary walked into the garage.

She retired after working for many years at the Pine Lawn Cleaners, and she owned a two story brick home at 3838 McRee Street, two blocks west of Grand Avenue in the Shaw neighborhood, where she supplemented her income by subletting three rooms to boarders on the top floor. For several years her grandson Robert and his sister Rhonda stayed at the home on weekdays while their father was at work. She was active socially as a member of the Eastern Star; spent many days doing volunteer work at the St. Louis Archdiocese and Cathedral on Lindell Avenue in the City as well as for local parish functions at St. Ambrose; and participated in the Democratic Party's election committees and voter registration drives. Her grandson Robert remembers her as a proud, hard-working woman, a devoted Christian, full of faith and spirit, who encouraged him to follow Jesus. Mary died in 1997 six days shy of her eighty-fifth birthday and is buried in Sts. Peter and Paul Cemetery, St. Louis, Missouri.

## Carmelo Monti (May 10, 1913 – June 17, 1933)

Carmelo was probably named for his maternal grandfather Carmelo Gianino, who arrived in St. Louis at the end of April 1913, just days before the baby boy's birth on May 10th. One genealogical oddity occurred in both the 1920 and 1930 St. Louis censuses when he was identified as female, a daughter to Eligio and Anna, presumably both mistakes made by two different census takers who heard the name and made the assumption that Carmelo was a girl's name.

As a sixteen-year-old in 1930 he worked as a clerk in a shoe factory, but by 1933 he was working as a clerk in a grocery store, which was the family run confectionery located on the first floor of the flat where they lived at 2427 Goode Avenue. His nephew Louis C. Monti wrote that young Carmelo had a clubfoot, raised pigeons on the roof of the building, was very religious, and was considered saintly. His brother Roy Monti said that Carmelo was a good ball player but was so crippled that he could not run bases. His sister Vera (Monti) Combevis said that "Mello" was her best friend when she was a child, that he was particularly nice to her, and that he was "good, like a priest" and did not deserve to die the way he did.

Carmelo was killed in a shootout with the police on Saturday, June 17, 1933 when he was twenty years old, although his age was erroneously stated to be nineteen. Over these 70-plus years since the incident, the story was not forgotten but details became fuzzy or misinterpreted by younger family members who did not live through the times. Eyewitness accounts varied considerably, both then and today. As such, two newspaper articles published the next day, one in the *St. Louis Post-Dispatch* and one in the *St. Louis Globe Democrat*, are the best sources for the story.

According to the *Post's* Sunday morning paper, officers Frank Munsil and Eugene Kavanaugh were walking their patrol through the neighborhood around 1:15 p.m. when they came upon an old touring car without license plates. Parked alongside was a sedan, and inside, seventeen-year-old Dominic Munti (*sic*) was napping. Kavanaugh described the scene. Munsil approached Dominic, asked him who owned the car, and "I heard him (Munsil) tell Dominic, 'You have to get a license for it, or keep it off the street.'

"Dominic told him: 'You can't (bother) me. I don't have to have a license unless I drive it and I'm not driving it. You're always picking on me.'

"He got out of the car and they scuffled. Carmelo (Monti) came to the front of the store and then ran back and got a baseball bat. He yelled and started at me with it.

"I grabbed for the bat and so did his mother (Sebastiana Monti) and sister, Dominica (Monti) who is 15 years old. We were all struggling for the bat when the shooting was going on. Dominic yelled for Carmelo to go into the store and get the pistol.

"Carmelo started in, but at the door he met his father (Eligio Louis Monti) coming out with a revolver. The father stood in the doorway and fired at Munsil. I think his first shot hit him, but Munsil got his revolver out and fired his after he was wounded.

"Munti (*sic*) fell down and dropped his revolver. Dominic ran over and picked it up and fired it until it was empty."

The *Globe's* version of the story was briefer. The patrolmen were concerned that the car might be stolen since it had no plates or city license, so Munsil questioned Dominick Munti (*sic*) who was in the car. After being interrogated for awhile, Dominick yelled, "You've been monkeying with me long enough," got out of the car, and began tussling with Munsil. Kavanaugh tried to separate them but Carmelo came out of the store and seized him. Munsil told Dominick he was under arrest, so Don broke away and ran into the store. When he returned he had a baseball bat. By then, his mother Anna and sister Dominica were outside. The four of them began struggling over the bat and Anna seized it. Kavanaugh thought she was going to use it on him, so he grabbed it from her. About that time, Louis Munti (*sic*) emerged from the store with a revolver and fired at Munsil, who returned the fire. Louis, who was wounded, fired four more shots but staggered back into the store. Munsil was wounded in the right groin. Dominick grabbed the

## YOUTH SLAIN, FATHER AND PATROLMAN SHOT IN DUEL

**Fray Starts When Officers Question Brother of Victim About Lack of License Plates on Auto.**

---

**FAMILY JOINS IN QUARREL**

---

**Eleven Bullets Are Exchanged in Battle After Parents Come on Scene with Pistol and Baseball Bat.**

**Newspaper Article – June 18, 1933**
*St. Louis Globe Democrat*
Photos identified as Carmelo Munti, Dominick Munti, Louis Munti and Patrolman Frank Munsil.

Images from microfilm provided by the St. Louis Public Library.

revolver and fired the last round. Munsil fired six shots total. Dominick charged that Munsil had slapped him during the interrogation and that he fired the first shot "without provocation." Kavanaugh was not injured but a bullet passed through his cap.

The Post continued with more details. Additional police officers arrived at the scene and subdued the "melee." Carmelo had been shot in the stomach and the right arm. Eligio was shot three times in the left arm and once in the chest. Munsil was wounded in the left shoulder. All three were taken seven blocks due west to old De Paul Hospital on North Kingshighway, and shortly thereafter Carmelo and Eligio were moved under guard to City Hospital where Carmelo died at 6:50 p.m., five and one-half hours after being wounded.

Meanwhile, Sebastiana, Dominic, and Dominica were hauled to the station for questioning. As Kavanaugh related the details of the incident to reporters, Dominica shouted her version of the story. "Butch fired the first shot," (she) insisted, referring to Munsil. "Carmelo was running into the store when Butch shot him, and he fell down in the store. My father had a pistol and Butch knew it so he shot him, too. Then my father took the pistol out and shot Butch and Butch shot him again."

**Newspaper Article – June 18, 1933**
*St. Louis Post-Dispatch*
Photos identified as Carmelo Munti, Louis Munti, and Patrolman Frank Munsil.

Images from microfilm provided by the St. Louis Public Library.

Dominic denied that he had shouted for Carmelo to get a pistol. "When I got out of the car," he said, "Butch clapped his hand on my neck, swung me around and slapped my face. Carmelo called to me to come where he was standing, and Butch drew his gun. When I picked up the revolver my father dropped I fired it only once. I pulled the trigger a couple of more times, but it just snapped. I don't think I hit anybody."

Kavanaugh never drew his own gun as he had been busy fighting with Sebastiana and Dominca over the bat. His hat was shot off his head but he was not injured. Further investigation at the scene disclosed "quantities of home brew and whiskey," and reports that the confectionery had been the site of frequent liquor raids. Oddly, the home addresses for both police officers were included at the end of the story.

One significant difference between these two newspaper versions of the event centers on who went inside the store to get the baseball bat. The Post said that it was Carmelo, but the Globe said that it was Dominic.

In modern versions of the tale, and of particular note, is the conspicuous absence of the baseball bat and both Sebastiana and Domenica (Babe). One such version of the story holds that Dominic lay asleep in the back seat of his convertible automobile, with his feet dangling outside. Two police officers arrived and shots were fired, which hit Don in the foot. Carmelo came hobbling out of the house and was shot in the stomach. He stumbled away and collapsed dead at the end of the block. Meanwhile, brothers Sam, Roy, and Frank Monti were at the scene and saw "Pops" (Eligio) firing back at the police, wounding one of them so severely that he later lost his arm. Eligio was shot six times and Sam was wounded too, requiring hospitalization for as much as six months. Uncles Ralph, Carmelo, and Sam Gianino planned to kill the Irish police officers but their sister (Carmelo's mother) Sebastiana stopped them.

Another version of the story has Don in his Buick, which was either missing a license plate or had an expired tag, when a police officer approached and hassled him about the plate. A fight ensued and shots were fired. "Pops" emerged from the house with his gun and began firing. Some of the brothers came outside during the exchange and Carmelo was shot in the stomach, stumbled away, collapsed, and died at the end of the block. Eligo was wounded. In that version, no mention was made of Don, Sam, or the police officer being wounded.

In yet another version, the police officer who shot them had been extorting bribes and they probably had an argument over it. A fourth version has someone snitching to the authorities about Eligio's bootlegging. Don confronted the person, police were called and shots fired. "Pops" was shot in the arm and he served a couple of months in jail over the incident.

Carmelo's Missouri death certificate #21561 lists his cause of death as, "Gun shot wound of abdomen; perforation of Intestine; general peritonitis; abdominal hemorrhage caused by bullet wound." It goes on to read, "Justifiable homicide," but does not mention the police. A book *In the Line of Duty* lists police officers killed in St. Louis while doing their job, and none was recorded for the period of 1932 to 1934, indicating that no police officer died during this event. Frank Munsil retired from the department and died from hypertension at age 66 in 1944. Eugene A. Kavanaugh died in 1939 at age 48 from a coronary embolism.

Louis C. Monti wrote that on the day Carmelo died, the pigeons flew away one last time and never returned. His mother Sebastiana placed a necklace made of $50 Double Eagle gold coins around the neck of a patron saint statue in St. Ambrose Church at the funeral before his burial at Sts. Peter and Paul Cemetery. Years later, as a coin collector, Charlie Monti recognized the coin in a book, realized the value of the necklace, and drove into the city to The Hill to see it, but it wasn't there. The church claimed they had no record of it. Over many years, as the price of gold soared and the numismatic value of Double Eagles rose, Charlie, who was already disillusioned with the Catholic Church, puzzled angrily over what had become of the necklace and who had it, and he fumed that its removal was disrespectful to his mother and the memory of his brother.

## Dominic Joseph Monti (May 21, 1916 – May 15, 2002)

Don became a "hoofer" when he learned to tap dance from a black neighbor while the family lived on Goode Avenue near Downtown St. Louis. He was the tallest of the men in the family and that served him well as he began a professional dancing career at age sixteen in the burlesque theaters, which thrived around St. Louis during the Great Depression. He became a dance instructor with the WPA (Works Progress Administration) where he met another instructor, Lona Bernice Sims. She was ten to fifteen years his senior and a real beauty, but his family never approved of the relationship. They were both great dancers, but she wanted to lead, so they did not dance well together. Don participated in a Dance-A-Thon that took place over six months, as various teams were eliminated from the competition. Eventually, the contest came down to Don and his partner squaring off against another team. Neither team would quit, so they agreed to split the prize money and flip a coin for the honor of taking First Place. Don lost the coin toss.

At seventeen, Don participated in a brawl with two St. Louis police officers that left his brother Carmelo dead and his father seriously injured from gunshot wounds on June 17, 1933. Hauled into the police station, he countered the police version of the event to newspaper reporters and part of his narration appeared in two St. Louis newspapers the next day. See Carmelo's biography for details.

During World War Two, he served in the Army and was sent to Tonapah, Nevada, where he provided the entertainment at the Officer's Club. Lona followed him west. Their son Louis C. Monti wrote, "My dad was the only soldier allowed to go home every night as my mother became quite popular with the officers and their wives." They had two sons, both born in Tonapah, which is a 204-mile drive northwest of Las Vegas. After the war they moved to Vegas where he became a professional dancer and occasionally went to Hollywood to perform. Like all of his siblings, Don was a gambler, so the city suited him. In December 1947, his beautiful wife was hit by a car and killed and his 2-1/2-year-old son Louis was injured.

Don did what most newly widowed fathers would have done — he moved back to his hometown to be near his parents and siblings for their support. The three of them lived at the house on Flad Avenue, sometimes upstairs with "Aunt Jay" (Josie) who helped to raise the two children, and sometimes downstairs with "Grandma" Sebastiana and Aunt Vera, "depending on who was fighting with who at the time."

For many years, Don and some of his brothers with their wives went dancing for their weekend entertainment, until nightclubs with dance floors began disappearing. His son Louis C. Monti wrote, "He would also take us fishing with Mozella and her son. Mozella was a very large 'Aunt Jemima' look-alike who worked in the restaurant (Pagliacci's on Kingshighway) where my father was maitre d' for many years. Pop was never a waiter. He did work as a parking lot attendant on the riverfront (near the Arch) and later (as a museum guard) at the St. Louis Art Museum (in Forest Park)." He loved beautiful things, including art, music, and women. He once introduced his two sons to Leroy Robert "Satchel" Paige, one of the few black baseball players during the 1940-1950 era before integration. Louis continued, "It's funny that my father, who generally was quite prejudiced, was on the individual level kind and compassionate."

Don clearly absorbed the harsh lessons of the Great Depression as he never bought things on credit, except his house at 5727 Potomac, which he bought around 1957 and paid off early. He drove used cars purchased with cash. Gambling was a lure, especially craps, but he preferred to bet with the house instead of throwing the dice himself. He always said, "Gambling money knows no home." Eventually he was busted in an FBI raid, sentenced to two years probation for illegal gaming, and prohibited from leaving the area during that time.

In 1954 he began seeing Mary, or Don's Mary, to distinguish her from his sister Mary, and she became his common-law wife. After Mary's death in 1997, he fell in love with Kay and they were together for two years until her death in 2000. Don developed prostate cancer, a tumor on his lung, and severely blocked arteries but refused to have surgery for any of it, which completely ruined his health and lead to great pain. "I don't want you to mourn me," he told Louis. "I've had three great loves in my life. Your mother, Mary, and Kay. That's three more than most people ever get." He died in 2002 just six days before his 86th birthday.

## Salvatore Joseph Arturo Monti (January 12, 1918 – October 21, 1962)

Like most of his sibling's names, by the 1920 St. Louis census, Sam's had already been abbreviated from his formal Italian given name Salvatore. Not long after the 1929 stock market crash, he had to drop out school after finishing sixth grade. He and his younger brother Charlie had grown up to be best buddies, so to escape their crowded house with four children to a bed, they both volunteered for the Civilian Conservation Corps (CCC) and went to work at Babler State Park during the Great Depression where they built a variety of structures, retaining walls, and roads and sent money home to help their parents.

By the time World War Two came along, Sam went his own way and enlisted in the Army, serving in the infantry assigned to General Patton's Third Armored Division, African Armored Corps, from 1942 in Morocco to Tunisia and Algeria; continuing with Patton in the Seventh Army for the invasion of Sicily in 1943 where they liberated Palermo, then Messina, the city closest to mainland Italy; then up through the boot of Italy with the Fifth Army and the bloody battles for Monte Cassino in 1944. He said that he was only scared once – "from the time he went down the netting into the landing craft off the coast of North Africa" until the time "he got off the boat in New York." Although he had seen killing from a distance, his first experience with death up-close-and-personal was when he saw a fourteen-year-old German boy killed at Monte Cassino. He told his son-in-law Tom Beishir that he "vomited violently" and was horrified because he had always loved children. Years later, after Sam's death, three pages of battle commendations were discovered attached to his discharge papers.

Returning home, Sam married Nellie Jane Charlton, who had a six-year-old daughter Joyce, born before the start of World War Two. He went to work for the City of St. Louis Street Department with his brother Roy as a curb setter — a hard, physically demanding job which involved placing long granite blocks to form curbing along the street's edge on thoroughfares all over the city. For a while he and his brother Charlie also owned a tavern in the City.

Together, Sam and Nellie had another daughter JoAnn and a son, Sam Jr. who did not survive infancy. Joyce and JoAnn were raised equally as Sam's daughters, and they never did without, although, "he didn't like to spend money for clothes (and) that was always a bone of contention with us girls." In spring 1956 when Tom went to pick up Joyce for their first date at her home on Magnolia, he received quite a surprise. Sam "was sitting on the couch in his underwear," and he commanded, "'Hold out your hands,' then he asked me if I liked them. When I said yes, he responded, 'Then you know where to keep them.'. . . I can't remember he and I having a cross word about anything from that time on." Sam was protective of and generous with everyone he loved; he made fabulous ravioli that he shared with all the family; but he "wouldn't give those he disliked the time of day." Tom said that when he and Joyce were first married, they struggled financially, especially after the births of their first two children, and Sam occasionally appeared at their door with a box full of groceries, handed it over and left.

Family folklore said that Sam was a bit wild; he and his brother Don were known to get together on the Fourth of July and New Years Eve and discharge their firearms into the night air. In a letter dated Dec. 22, 1948, his brother Charlie wrote to his wife Mickey, "Sunday nite after the dance was over at Joe's, Sam had an accident. He sure was drunk and Vera got hurt a little but not much to talk about, anyway that's what Mom was telling me. Boy I won't ride with him." Recently, Vera said that she did not recall this event, which happened over fifty years ago, so in all likelihood, the story was exaggerated, as seems to be the case in general regarding Sam and alcohol. While everyone agrees that he did drink more than most of his siblings, his daughter Joyce wrote, "Too much emphasis is put on his drinking. His drinking did not cause family problems that I can remember, the only work he ever missed was due to the weather, being his was an outside job." Instead, he is remembered by those closest to him as "a good man" who was "generous to a fault."

Sam developed a rare form of acute myelogenous leukemia, which in those days was largely untreatable and patients typically lived only a year or so. He died at age forty-four on October 21, 1962, which was the same day that his son Sam Jr. had been born in 1950. Nelly developed colon cancer and died just two years later on October 25, 1964, the same day that Sam Jr. died. Tom said, "They died too young, but there is a living legacy they left behind that can never be taken away from them. There is Joyce, JoAnn, four grandsons, twelve great grandchildren, three great-great grandchildren, and two more great-great grandchildren on the way. . . we miss them a lot." They are buried together in Resurrection Cemetery, St. Louis, Missouri.

## Dominica Marie (Monti) Marku (April 24, 1919 – October 9, 1986)

Identified on two St. Louis censuses as Dominica or Dominika, she was called Babe all of her life and was the youngest daughter in the family for nine years, until her sister Vera was born in 1928. As a fifteen-year-old, she participated in a brawl with two St. Louis police officers that left her brother Carmelo dead and her father seriously injured from gunshot wounds. Hauled into the police station, she bravely countered the police version of the event to newspaper reporters and her narration appeared in the *St. Louis Post-Dispatch* the next day. See Carmelo's biography for more detail. Somehow, she emerged from that trauma with a sparkling, energetic *joie de vivre*, a desire to live life to the fullest, and was clearly one of the most entrepreneurial siblings in the family.

Around 1940 she married Buck Hendricks, and her nephew Carmelo L. Monti said that her brothers "took quickly to Buck, considered him one of their own, and never seemed to accept Babe's position or reasons for dumping him" when the couple divorced. Tired of the criticism, she moved to Chicago to pursue an independent life. For a while she worked as a Playboy Bunny in the Chicago Playboy Club, so there is no doubt she was an attractive, charismatic woman. Another nephew Louis C. Monti recalled that in 1949 as a four-year-old child he stayed with her in the back room of her neighborhood beauty shop on the north side of Chicago. Sometime during the 1950s she married Fred Sykes but the marriage did not last, and many years later she told Louis that divorcing Sykes had been a sad mistake. Around 1960 she met Jack Marku, who Carmelo described as "an astute, hustling, entrepreneurial person with a lot of business sense," and who Louis described as "a wonderful man who took very good care of Aunt Babe and always welcomed her family to their home."

Tiring of the harsh Chicago winters, they relocated to Las Vegas, where she opened another beauty salon called "Marie's" on Torrey Pines Drive, while Jack went to work at the casinos servicing slot machines and transporting cash as a "bagman." They had no children of their own. When Babe came to St. Louis to visit her family around Christmas, she overcompensated and showered her nieces and nephews with lavish gifts, then looked for the next poker game to recoup her expenses. Carmelo observed, "Between Babe and Mary there was no lack of activity or noise around the place. She was known to hold her own with the brothers with her colorful use of language and reliance on 'Luck' in the way the 'old Italians' saw superstition and luck as a part of life." Louis said that Babe was intuitive and would have been considered "gifted" in the Old World. Her house in Las Vegas was filled with many objects from a wide range of friends who loved her as she "had a wonderful gift of being able to make people laugh."

Unfortunately, Babe's intensity had a dark side. She gambled too much, drank every day, smoked excessively, and had a kleptomania problem of shoplifting small things like salt-and-pepper shakers from restaurants. She developed lung cancer, perhaps from smoking, perhaps from inhaling too many chemicals in her beauty shop. "When she found out she had cancer, she flew to Santa Fe (where Louis lived) twenty-two times in the two years before her death. She was dearly loved and was an inspiration to many people. She had an uncanny ability to meet people in (his) restaurant and be a comfort to them. . . She died without fear and with dignity as befitting a GREAT LADY."

**Note:** In photograph to the right, woman identified as Vera Monti (age 15) has also been identified as perhaps Dominica (Babe) Monti (age 24).

**Flad Avenue House Front Porch in 1943**
Standing Left to Right: Charlie, Vera, and Sam Monti
Seated: Kathleen and Mary (Monti) Viviano
Photograph courtesy of Milda (Kaempfe) Monti Estate

## Sebastiano (Charles) Joseph Monti Sr. (November 28, 1920 – June 27, 2006)

Charlie was named Sebastiano Joseph as a baby, but by the 1930 St. Louis census his name appeared as Charles, and everyone called him Charlie his entire life. When the Social Security Administration required him to choose a name at retirement, he chose Charles.

As a teenager, he worked for Shenandoah Pie Company delivering pies to restaurants at 4:00 a.m. and he sold newspapers. Later, he joined the Civilian Conservation Corps (CCC) with his older brother Sam, and they worked at Babler State Park during the Great Depression where they built a variety of structures, retaining walls, and roads. Life was difficult for his large family with so many young children, so he did what he could to help his parents but still managed to graduate high school.

He loved playing baseball, softball, and boxing when he could find an opponent. Other kids with whom he played ball included Joe Garagiola and Lawrence "Yogi" Berra, who lived on The Hill on Elizabeth Avenue within blocks of his home. When scouts for the minor league farm camps offered positions to him, Joe, and Yogi, Charlie had to turn them down because he could not scrape together

the money to pay for his slot. His friends received $500 bonuses so money was not an issue for them. Both went on to have long running, acclaimed careers in Major League baseball. Ironically, Joe later commented that Yogi and others in his neighborhood were better ball players than he was, and Charlie agreed with him. He remained a baseball fan his entire life and spent many happy hours playing a variety of sports with his six children, including his only daughter Sheila.

Around 1940, after completing the CCC, he "rode the rails" out to California. He loved Seal Beach and reminisced fondly of his "hobo days," calling them the best days of his life. During World War Two in 1942, he joined the Navy, perhaps influenced by his father's experience. "I wanted to go into the Navy all my life," he told a newspaper reporter for the *South County Journal* in 2004. After boot camp in San Diego, California as a Petty Officer First Class he became a cook and was assigned to the *USS Block Island CVE 21*, a "baby flattop" aircraft carrier converted from a tanker and small by today's standards. After crossing through the Panama Canal, his carrier traveled the Atlantic with five destroyers, hunted German U-Boats, and sank two of them. Their ship was the first to use airborne rockets against submarines. On May 29, 1944, between the Canary and Azores Islands, three torpedoes hit the carrier, putting the crew into the water. The sneaky U-Boat captain moved his submarine under the sinking ship, so the destroyers could not locate him. While they searched, Charlie floated in the water, awaiting rescue amidst oil slicks and debris, as torpedoes hit one of the destroyers and depth charges exploded. Uninjured, he received a month's leave then went to Tacoma, Washington where he and the entire crew boarded a new ship – the *USS Block Island CVE 106*. Out in the Pacific, the ship was the first to have an all-Marine group flying the first night missions. They went to Honolulu, Guam, and the Philippines. After bombing missions all over the Pacific, they rescued 1,200 POWs from Formosa, some "walking skeletons" from the Bataan Death March. Traveling again through the Panama Canal and after docking in New York, he was discharged on November 5, 1945. Later in life, Charlie enjoyed the camaraderie of fellow shipmates as they met annually for reunions, even hosting one such event in St. Louis.

From the East Coast he rode the train back home to St. Louis. After the holidays, his brother Salvatore's fiancé Jane introduced him to one of her friends, Milda "Mickey" Kaempfe, and six months later on July 6, 1946 Mickey and Charlie were married by a justice of the peace in St. Charles, Missouri. This caused a great row in the Monti family, since he had dared to marry a non-Catholic who was not Italian, but soon enough, Mickey won them over with her sweet nature and the family accepted her.

After their first son was born in 1947, the couple disagreed on how to have him baptized — Catholic or Lutheran. After their second son was born just eleven months later, Mickey relented and told Charlie he could have them baptized Catholic. A priest refused to baptize the babies until the young couple married in the Catholic Church. Charlie was furious and declared that Mickey could raise her children as Lutheran, which she did. In a letter dated Dec. 22, 1948 he wrote to his "Dearest Darling" Mickey who was in Frohna with their two young sons, "You can have the baby's (Butch and Carmelo) baptized so I guess that gets some off your mind."

Charlie and Mickey briefly went to California (some think for vacation, others say to relocate) but returned to St. Louis (some said when news of his mother's heart problems reached them, but others believed their return was due to her pregnancy and eminent delivery date). They moved several times, from an apartment on Kingshighway to a flat in North St. Louis on Labadie Avenue not far from Goode, close to Sportsman's Park (the first of three Busch Stadiums) where he occasionally went to watch a baseball game, and finally to their first home at 5116 Michael Avenue in Shrewsbury, Missouri.

Charlie spent most of his life working as a lithographer for the American Can Company and serving as a Union Shop Steward. The quality of his work was so highly regarded that he was always given the four-color printing jobs, was sent to New York to learn how to operate the first seamless aluminum can press in St. Louis, and was offered relocation to Puerto Rico to oversee that plant's seamless operation, which he turned down. His job with the Union required him to advocate on behalf of his fellow members with Management, and he stood up for black members in equal measure, to such an extent that white members once threatened to have him removed from the role. He used his influence to obtain jobs for his brother-in-law Reiney Kaempfe, nephew Courtney Meyer, and several of his sons as they worked their way through college.

The lithography job was physically demanding, required him to mix and stir thick ink, climb onto tall printing presses to pour the ink into vats, and then get back down. Most times, he jumped. After he developed a herniated disc, he once told this author that it probably was due to so many years of jumping onto the factory's concrete floor, although other family members recall a specific incident that involved the strain of breaking loose a press that was locked in place. After back surgery in 1978, he could no longer work and was placed on disability.

**Charles Monti with his parents Eligio and Sebastiana (Gianino) Monti in 1943**
Photograph courtesy of Rob Willis

A second surgery for prostate cancer left him with debilitating side effects. He remained active, despite the pain from both surgeries, but it wore his patience thin, so his native hot temper was easily sparked. After he developed problems with his heart, he refused to slow down and, being as tough as nails, often swore, "I'm gonna outlive all you sons-of-bitches."

He and Mickey worked side-by-side maintaining their home and yards, and he spent as much time in the kitchen cooking as she did. His Christmas pies and Italian rolled meatloaf were renowned. When his son's wife Kathy required numerous hospitalizations, they stepped in and helped to raise their two grandchildren, devoting much of their later years to managing a second household for them, taking them to and from school, and feeding them most days.

Like most of his siblings, Charlie liked to gamble. When his six children were young, he would gather everyone into the car and drive 1,600 miles (each way) to Las Vegas, once stopping only to sleep for four hours behind a gas station; but other times stopping in a motel overnight halfway there. Many times, he won enough money playing the Craps and Blackjack tables to extend their stay, pay for the motels and food for the large group, and come home happy. Other times, he lost and no one was happy. Throughout the years, the couple continued to make trips to Las Vegas, usually flying and staying in "comped" hotels, arrangements courtesy of "pit bosses," whom Charlie befriended while playing Craps. After gambling was legalized in Mississippi, they rode the bus to Tunica on short day-trips or weekends, occasionally traveling with Charlie's brother Roy and his wife Catherine.

Charlie had an entrepreneurial bent and exercised it by dealing in coins. Like his brother Frank, he collected coins, but more than anything, he loved the thrill of buying cheap and selling high. Another favorite activity was playing pool, which he learned to play and hustle as a young man. After he and Mickey moved into their new house at 10520 Gregory Court in 1977, about a half-mile from his brother Frank's home on Carolynne Drive, he bought a pool table for the basement, where he taught his children and grandchildren to play the game. He enjoyed demonstrating his skills by making difficult bank shots. Sometimes they wagered on a game, and Charlie often won, but he was the first to return his winnings. All of his children remember his generosity in sharing his time with them, the many sacrifices he and Milda made to give them a good life, and his great sense of humor and wit.

Milda and Charles just missed enjoying their 60th wedding anniversary on July 6, 2006 because Charlie died on June 27th from heart failure brought on by aspirating pneumonia. As a veteran, he is buried in Jefferson Barracks National Cemetery, St. Louis, Missouri, along with Mickey, and leaves behind six children, six grandchildren, three adopted grandchildren, five step-grandchildren, and many, many great-grandchildren.

## Frank Monti (June 15, 1922 — April 11, 1924)

Little Frankie died as a toddler. He was born on June 15, 1922 at 5242 Wilson Avenue and died there on April 11, 1924. His doctor attended him from April 7 until his death from acute bronchitis complicated by bronchial pneumonia. The only known photograph of him was made with his family in 1922 or 1923 while he was a baby seated on his father Eligio's lap, shown on the cover and inside cover.

## Francisco Carmelo Monti (May 15, 1924 — August 11, 2011)

As a teenager, Frank attended Ranken Technical College on Finney Avenue in St. Louis near the Central West End for two years from 1939 to 1941. A couple of years later, as World War Two was intensifying, he left home and joined the U.S. Coast Guard where he served for three years. Although the Coast Guard's roll was crucial for defending America's shoreline from enemy submarines, his brothers liked to tease Frank about not seeing any "real" war. Despite the teasing, they treasured his ability to keep "tabs" and in touch with them when they made it back to the States. Charlie said that Frank always seemed to know when they were in ports-of-call, and he remembered running into Frank in Times Square in New York City unexpectedly when he and his sailor buddies were on shore leave. He said that it happened again in Norfolk, Virginia.

After the War, Frank returned to St. Louis in 1946 where he met Faye Barbee on a blind date that had been arranged by his cousin's friend Ruth Smith. They were married on July 5, 1947, the day before his brother Charlie's first wedding anniversary. He and Fay moved to Chicago where he passed his GED tests at Woodrow Wilson College (now Kennedy-King College), and he sold televisions while attending class on the GI bill. After college he went to work for Vickers Electric, then McDonnell Douglas (now Boeing) where he worked for many years as an electrical engineer until his retirement. His family moved a lot because of his career. After Chicago, they went to Alamogordo, New Mexico; then back to the St. Louis area in St. Ann; then St. Louis; and finally to a great house on Carolynne in Sappington, Missouri with a swimming pool where they hoped to stay. Frank's job required that they move again, so they rented out the house as they left for Ellicot City, Maryland (near Baltimore), then South Windsor, Connecticut (near Hartford).

During those years, Frank said that his most memorable events were having his three children (two sons and a daughter) born from 1952 to 1959. Finally, around 1968, they returned to their home in Sappington where they remained. In the old days, Frank and Faye, along with Charlie and his wife Milda, and Roy and his wife Catherine often went out dancing together, and Frank called himself "FFF," a self-proclaimed nickname meaning "fastest feet on the floor." Like his siblings, he enjoyed gambling and made frequent trips to Las Vegas, sometimes in their company. As his granddaughter Erin reports, he was "a Taurus in every sense of the word — stubborn and hard-headed," sounding very much like some of the other Monti siblings. Unlike many of his siblings, he had no interest in sports and once fell asleep at a hockey game. For awhile, he repaired televisions for family members; he once owned a family-run pizza parlor, which was successful until a fire destroyed it; he enjoyed making extra cash doing odd-jobs like operating a gum-ball machine route; and he actively worked at collecting coins, a hobby he once shared with Charlie.

Over the decades, he drove a few different cars — a new 1955 Oldsmobile, a 1962 Pontiac Tempest station wagon, a Toyota van, a Toyota Cressida, and a 2003 Chevy Malibu. He liked to entertain his family of three adult children and five grandchildren; kept a "ton of food (around the house) for the grandkids"; and, like several of his siblings, cooked a fabulous rolled, Sicilian meatloaf with sauce for the crowd. At Christmas, his favorite tradition for over sixty-five years was to bake at least ten kinds of cookies. He particularly enjoyed "spoiling his wife," loved his family, especially his grandchildren, and as granddaughter Erin said, "Overall, he's a very kind man." After settling back in St. Louis around 1968, his family joined Seven Holy Founders Catholic Church on Rock Hill at Gravois in Affton, and Frank — as one of the most religious of all the siblings who went to Mass even in Las Vegas — faithfully attended Novenas every Tuesday. He was a member of American Legion Post #300 and the Knights of Columbus Rosati Council #795, and he's buried in Jefferson Barracks National Cemetery, St. Louis County, Missouri.

## Rosario Guiseppe Monti (February 21, 1926 – April 2011)

Like most of his siblings, Rosario's given name was anglicized and he became Roy Joseph to most people, as early as the 1930 St. Louis census when he was only four years old. As a seven-year-old boy he witnessed the shooting death of his older brother Carmelo, "a scene I will never forget," he wrote. After attending Roosevelt High School for one year, he dropped out in 1941 at age fifteen so he could go to work at the Central Counter Company making shoe parts to help with his family's finances. He met his future wife Catherine Banker while working there.

As World War Two progressed, he joined the U.S. Navy, and following Boot Camp, he and Catherine were married before he shipped out. He served aboard two tank and troop carriers — *LST 211* and *LST 265* — and went to the Mediterranean — Algeria and Tunisia in Africa; Palermo, Sicily; Marseilles, France; Casa Blanca, Morocco; and Florence, Italy — many of the same places his brother Sam was seeing while in the Army. By the time the war was over, he had become a Motor Machinist 3rd Class Petty Officer.

Back home in St. Louis, he and Catherine were the witnesses at his brother Charlie's wedding on July 6, 1946 in St. Charles, Missouri, and he recalled that they had to cross the old, narrow, fire-prone wooden bridge over the Missouri River to get there, "and we all survived!"

The next year, he and Sam went to work as curb setters, a hard, physically demanding job which involved placing long granite blocks to form curbing along the street's edge on thoroughfares all over the city. He worked two jobs for a while — setting curbs during the day, then working the night shift in the Hyde Park Brewery where Carling made Stag Beer, their most popular brand. Eventually he worked his way up to being Foreman, and finally Superintendent as the head of the Refuse Division for the City of St. Louis Street Department, where, he quipped, "I (was) responsible for having (picked up) every trashcan in the city, not a small feat." An in-the-trenches sort of guy, he lost the ring figure from his left hand when his wedding band was caught on a hook and yanked off as a dump truck pulled away. He had worked for the Department for forty-one years when he retired at age sixty-two in 1988. Over those years, he owned "every car imaginable" including a Packard, Chevy, Ford, Oldsmobile, Buick, and finally, his favorite car, a Toyota, so reliable he "hasn't spent a dime on it in ten years."

Roy's nephew Carmelo L. Monti recalls that his uncle was an exceedingly independent person, liked to socialize, had a sense of humor, and loved clowning around. "In the old days he was always ready to get together for parties and picnics. He and his wife Catherine often joined with Lou and Jane, Joe's son and his wife, and sometimes Sammy Gianino and Vi, for a night out on the town. Roy, like Sam, liked to indulge, often preferring a bottle of J & B or Dewers Scotch, or Bloody Mary's to that of a shot of bourbon whiskey." Roy's brother Charlie called him "Racetrack Harry" because the group of them spent so much time together betting on horse races at Cahokia Downs and Fairmount Park in Illinois.

Roy and Catherine had three children, and one of their great sorrows in life was when they lost their middle child, daughter Catherine Mary, in September 1997 just a month before her 49th birthday. "It was a terrible loss." At the time of writing in 2009, they had twelve grandchildren and twenty great-grandchildren "with two more on the way."

In 2009, Roy was in declining health with tumors on his kidneys, but he continued to care for Catherine who had Alzheimer's. The couple had just celebrated their 65th wedding anniversary when he wrote, "and they said it wouldn't last," with his typical touch of humor. Despite their ailments, they still had fun with Roy's sister Vera aboard the Ameristar Casino located in St. Charles on the Missouri River, below the Blanchette Bridge, two giant steel and concrete cantilever spans — a big improvement over the old wooden bridge they once crossed to "stand up" for his brother Charlie. Roy and Catherine died within a few months of each other in 2011.

## Veronica Mary (Monti) Combrevis (1928)

Although Veronica appears by her given name as a two-year-old child on the 1930 St. Louis census, she has been called Vera all of her life. At seventeen, she went to work on the assembly line at the Prince Gardener factory making wallets and billfolds. As the youngest sibling, indeed the youngest daughter born nine years after her next oldest sister Babe, she became the "mother's-helper" in the family after her older sisters left home to marry and, especially after her father Eligio died on December 24, 1951.

Vera wrote that as a young woman "I loved to dance and tried to go dancing every chance I had on Friday and Saturday nights at Casa Loma Ballroom (on Iowa Avenue in South St. Louis) where I met my (future) husband Leonard Combrevis. My brothers were very protective of me and greeted him with rifles loaded to make sure he only had good intentions toward me. It didn't scare him off though — he kept on coming around. He scared me at first though, with his long sideburns and Harley (motorcycle) he drove but convinced me four years later to marry him on May 7, 1955 at St. Margaret of Scotland." Leonard was a truck driver when they first met, but he went to night school, was hired by McDonnell Douglas, and eventually worked his way up to being a supervisor.

As newlyweds, the couple lived at the Monti family home at 4131 Flad Avenue where Vera continued to help her mother Sebastiana while beginning her own family of six, first with Linda then Julia. That house was sold in 1958 and the couple bought their own first house on Raywood in Affton, taking Anna (whose health was failing) with them. As Vera's duties as caregiver for her mother increased, her own family continued to grow with the births of Louis and Leonard Jr. Anna mellowed with age and delighted in her grandchildren filling up the house. Eight years later "and running out of room" the whole family moved one last time to their home on Tioga Court in Sunset Hills and two more sons came along — Jeffrey and Vincent. "Mom died (November 3, 1966) shortly after our move and was greatly missed."

Leonard worked evenings from 3 to 11 p.m. for many years while the children were in elementary school so Vera was kept busy with six active, growing children, as she took them to school, sporting events and Scouts. After Jeffrey and Vincent entered school, she found time to volunteer and also work in the school cafeteria "which I loved." With one special-needs child and another who suffered a catastrophic automobile accident as a young man, Vera devoted her time and energy to being a nurturing, loving mother, so all of her children flourished.

Vera and Leonard enjoyed traveling and around their 24th wedding anniversary, they took their first Caribbean cruise. Other favorite memories include an Alaskan cruise, a trip to Hawaii, and, best of all, touring Italy. In 2001 Leonard was diagnosed with lung cancer, but he was determined to survive until they could celebrate their 50th wedding anniversary, which they did on May 7, 2005. Leonard succumbed just three weeks later on May 31.

Since then, Vera keeps busy maintaining their home in Sunset Hills, where she looks forward to planting flowers in the spring, "anything that blooms." She likes watching football on television, noting that "my all-time favorite player (was) Joe Montana." With six grandchildren and three great-grandchildren, she still devotes much of her time to family, including helping her daughter Linda occasionally baby-sit two great-granddaughters and hosting a big Christmas Day dinner.

With nearly forty years of membership at St. Catherine Laboure Parish on Sappington Road, she is involved in the Women's Guild, which holds fundraising events for the church and the needy, and recently she began "volunteering at Hosea House (a homeless shelter on Gravois Avenue in the City) on Monday mornings with my neighbors" where she sorts and hangs donated clothing that is distributed to the needy. She enjoys the camaraderie of all the people, both her fellow volunteers and the people who come in seeking help, regardless of race or creed, as she continues her lifelong tradition of providing care to those around her.

**Monti Family Gathering circa 1955 to 1960**
Photograph courtesy of Rob Willis

# Chapter Five

## ITALIAN NAMES:
## DEMOGRAPHICS, ETYMOLOGY AND TRADITIONS

### Demographics

Given all of the surnames found in these pages, a brief mention of their demographics in Sicily is appropriate. In 2003, an Internet site listed 390 towns in Sicily and itemized the names of all their citizens. Augusta had about 34,000 citizens, and Catania was ten times larger with about 342,000. In Augusta, about 1% of the entire population, or 382, had the surname Gianino. Fourteen other towns had citizens named Gianino, but only a few were in each town. There were 523 total, island-wide. Almost certainly, the name originated in or near Augusta, and it remains a significant name there to this day. This differs greatly from the name Giannino (with two n's). They were more widely scattered, found in 34 towns, but mostly in Messina and Catania. None were in Augusta.

The name Monti appeared 948 times and Monte, 1144 times, and they differed only slightly in their distribution. Monti was found in 43 towns, in eight provinces, but most were concentrated in the region in and around Palermo. There were 101 in the province of Catania. With slightly more numbers, Monte was found in 58 towns, in nine provinces, and they were even more concentrated in the region around Palermo. There were 122 in the province of Catania. Therefore, Eligio's last name, spelled Monte with an "e" on the ships' registries but with an "i" on later documents, could easily have been spelled either way, further complicating any effort to find his parents or adoptive parents.

The name Daniele (647) occurred in 31 towns, in eight provinces, but the largest concentration (109) lived in the town of Augusta. Another 86 live in the surrounding province of Siracusa. The next largest concentration (132) were in the province of Catania. The surname Balsano (675) occurred almost exclusively in Palermo. However, a more common spelling Balsamo (3,505) occurred island-wide in 96 towns, with large numbers in every major city. The heaviest concentration was in Catania. Finally, there were 473 people in Augusta with the name Passanisi, which is similar to the Passanese who formed the fruit business with Gianino in Boston.

## Etymology

The historical origins of names also provide some interesting insights. As mentioned in the first chapter, many ancient civilizations colonized Sicily, but names for the Monti ancestors appear to derive from just a few groups including Jewish, Roman, and Spanish, with Hebrew, Latin, and Spanish being the most influential early languages.

## Given Names Include:

**Carmelo** – Spanish masculine form of Carmel, from the title of Mary 'Our Lady of Carmel'. Carmel (meaning "garden" in Hebrew) is a mountain in Israel mentioned in the Old Testament. It was the site of several Christian monasteries.

**Eligio** - the Italian form of the Late Latin name Eligius, which was derived from the Latin word *eligere* "to choose." The 7th Century Saint Eligius is the patron saint of metalworkers.

**Santa** – Feminine form of Santo, which is the Italian form of the Late Latin name Sanctius, which was derived from the word *sanctus* meaning "saintly, holy."

**Sebastiana** – Feminine form of Sebastian, from the Roman name Sebastianus which meant "from Sebastia" in Latin. Sebastia was a town in Asia Minor, its name deriving from Greek *sebastos* "venerable." Saint Sebastian was a 3rd-century Roman soldier martyred by arrows after it was discovered he was a Christian. This was also the name of a king of Portugal who died in a crusade against Morocco.

## Surnames include:

**BALSANO** – (more commonly spelled BALSAMO) – from Hebrew, Greek and Latin meaning "spice."

**DANIELE** – Italian form of Daniel, from the Hebrew name Daniyel meaning, "God is my judge." Daniel was a Hebrew prophet whose story is told in the Book of Daniel in the Old Testament. He lived during the Jewish captivity in Babylon, where he served in the court of the king, rising to prominence by interpreting the king's dreams. The book also presents Daniel's four visions of the end of the world.

**GIANINO** – And **GIANNINO** - From the first name Gianni, an abbreviation of Giovanni, which is derived from the Hebrew Yohanan, consisting of Yahweh meaning "God", and *hanan* meaning "to be merciful," combining to mean "Merciful God "

**MONTE or MONTI** – Italian, Monte is singular, Monti is plural; it means "Mount"; hence, Monte Etna is singular, but mountain ranges are called Monti. As a surname, it means "coming from the mountain(s)."

## Traditions

Old World naming traditions carried through to lesser or greater degrees in America, depending on the family and how closely they stayed within their ethnic communities. In Italy, the firstborn son was named for his paternal grandfather; the second, for his maternal grandfather; the third for his father; and the fourth for his paternal great-grandfather. Additional sons were given the names of paternal or maternal granduncles in alternating sequence. If the firstborn son was given a Christian Saint's name instead of his paternal grandfather's name, then the second son took the name of his father instead of his maternal grandfather's name. If the father died before the birth of any child, then the newborn was named for the deceased parent.

This explains why all the Gianino and some Monti given names seem to repeat. Since Arturo Monte (*sic*) was probably the firstborn son for Eligio and Sebastiana, if they followed the above rules, then Arturo Monte must also be the name of Eligio's father. This offers a clue for future research into the mysterious origins of the Monte line in Catania, Sicily. Further, their second born son should have been named Carmelo, after Sebastiana's father. Instead, he was called Joseph Louis. Perhaps Eligio wanted to give that son a Saint's name and added his own middle name Louis, since he was often called Luigi or Louis himself. Under the Old World rules, succeeding names would have been derived from granduncles, alternating between paternal and maternal sides, but Eligio was an orphan and likely knew of no brothers. The next baby boy Carmelo was more likely named after his maternal grandfather Carmelo Gianino who arrived in St. Louis at the end of April 1913 just days before Carmelo's birth on May 10th. (The names Louis and Carmelo were carried forward to several descendants, including Carmelo Louis Monti and Louis Carmelo Monti.) Continuing with the naming tradition, Sebastiana likely chose two of her own brothers' names for her remaining boys, Salvatore and Sebastiano Charles. Origin of the names Dominic and Francisco are impossible to even guess, but recalling Ellis Island records, those names appeared numerous times for Gianino men heading from Sicily to Boston or St. Louis.

Trinacria

In the 3rd century BC the island of Sicily was called Thrinakie, meaning "Isle with Triangle's Form." Its shape, beautiful shores, and dangerous Monte Etna inspired this heraldic symbol illustrated by the head of Medussa surrounded by three shapely female legs. Today, the symbol is known as the Trinacria, and the Region of Sicily uses a stylized, friendlier version on a split yellow and red ground for it's official banner.

*Note:
### Santa Gianino's Ancestry
Santa's father was listed as Dominic Gianino of Augusta, Sicily, Italy by Pete Gianino on Santa's Missouri death certificate. Her mother's name was listed as unknown.

See page 10 for additional information about other potential Gianino family members who might provide clues for Santa's ancestry.

# Chapter Six

## DESCENDANTS OF PIETRO GIANINO

1. Pietro GIANINO (Augusta,Siracusa,Sicily,Italy)

  sp: Sebastiana DANIELE (Augusta,Siracusa,Sicily,Italy)

    2. Carmelo GIANINO (b.24 Nov 1865-Augusta,Siracusa,Sicily,Italy;d.13 Apr 1920-St. Louis,MO)

      sp: Santa GIANINO (b.5 Oct 1866-Augusta,,Sicily,Italy;m.Abt 1885;d.23 Dec 1955-St. Louis,MO) (See *Note page 52)

        3. Sebastiana GIANINO (b.25 Sep 1886-Augusta,Siracusa,Sicily,Italy;d.13 Nov 1966-St. Louis,MO)

          sp: Eligio Louis MONTI(MONTE) (b.5 Feb 1877-Catania,Catania,Italy;m.1 Dec 1901;d.24 Dec 1951-St. Louis,MO)

            4. Arturo Gianino MONTI (b.Abt Oct 1903-Augusta,Siracusa,Sicily,Italy;d.Bef 1910-St. Louis,MO)

            4. Joseph (Joe) Louis MONTI (b.14 Sep 1908-St. Louis,MO;d.22 May 1998-Glencoe,MO)

              sp: Theresa GENONI (b.18 Sep 1910;d.8 Jan 1988-St. Louis,MO)

                5. Louis R. MONTI (b.22 Mar 1928;d.24 Mar 1989-St. Louis,MO)

                  sp: Jane (?)

                    6. Deborah J. MONTI

                      sp: Thomas M. HADICAN

                    6. Diane MONTI

                5. Donna Marie MONTI

                  sp: Ed SCHMITT

                    6. Joey SCHMITT

                    6. Denise SCHMITT

                    6. Darlyn SCHMITT

            4. Josephine (Josie) Theresa MONTI (b.4 Jul 1910-St. Louis,MO;d.Jun 1996-St. Louis,MO)

              sp: Santo GIANINO (b.8 Oct 1901;d.Apr 1974-St. Louis,MO)

                5. Sam GIANINO

                  sp: Viola GUTWEILER (b.31 Jul 1931;d.1 Dec 2002-St. Louis,MO)

                    6. Stephen GIANINO

                      sp: Mary Stephanie SUM (d.2004)

                      7. Dominic GIANINO

                      7. Rebecca GIANINO

                  6. Paula GIANINO

                  6. Sam GIANINO

                  6. Louis GIANINO

                  6. John GIANINO

                    sp: Michelle (?)

                  6. Theresa GIANINO

            4. Maria (Mary) Margaret MONTI (b.22 Apr 1912-St. Louis,MO;d.16 Apr 1997-Warrenton,MO)

              sp: Anthony VIVIANO Jr. (m.(Div))

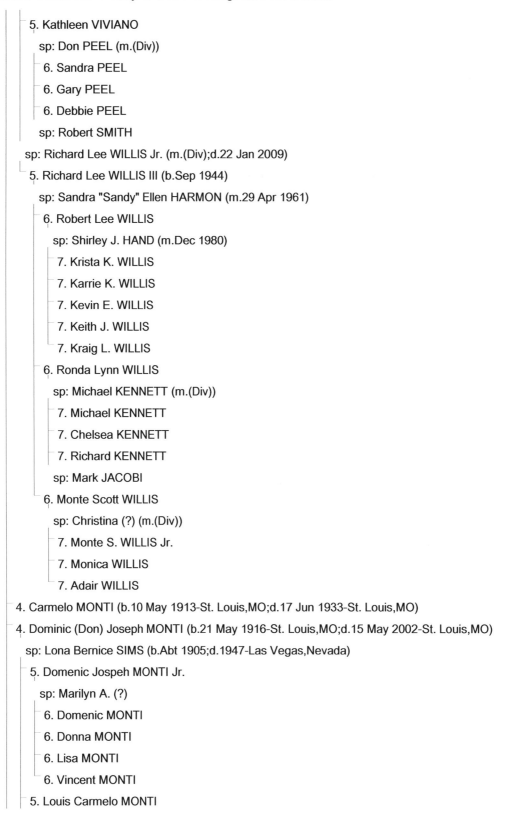

5. Kathleen VIVIANO

  sp: Don PEEL (m.(Div))

  6. Sandra PEEL

  6. Gary PEEL

  6. Debbie PEEL

  sp: Robert SMITH

sp: Richard Lee WILLIS Jr. (m.(Div);d.22 Jan 2009)

5. Richard Lee WILLIS III (b.Sep 1944)

  sp: Sandra "Sandy" Ellen HARMON (m.29 Apr 1961)

  6. Robert Lee WILLIS

    sp: Shirley J. HAND (m.Dec 1980)

    7. Krista K. WILLIS

    7. Karrie K. WILLIS

    7. Kevin E. WILLIS

    7. Keith J. WILLIS

    7. Kraig L. WILLIS

  6. Ronda Lynn WILLIS

    sp: Michael KENNETT (m.(Div))

    7. Michael KENNETT

    7. Chelsea KENNETT

    7. Richard KENNETT

    sp: Mark JACOBI

  6. Monte Scott WILLIS

    sp: Christina (?) (m.(Div))

    7. Monte S. WILLIS Jr.

    7. Monica WILLIS

    7. Adair WILLIS

4. Carmelo MONTI (b.10 May 1913-St. Louis,MO;d.17 Jun 1933-St. Louis,MO)

4. Dominic (Don) Joseph MONTI (b.21 May 1916-St. Louis,MO;d.15 May 2002-St. Louis,MO)

  sp: Lona Bernice SIMS (b.Abt 1905;d.1947-Las Vegas,Nevada)

  5. Domenic Jospeh MONTI Jr.

    sp: Marilyn A. (?)

    6. Domenic MONTI

    6. Donna MONTI

    6. Lisa MONTI

    6. Vincent MONTI

  5. Louis Carmelo MONTI

sp: Sonja (?) (m.(Div))

sp: Mary (?)

4. Salvatore (Sam) Joseph Arturo MONTI (b.12 Jan 1918-St. Louis,MO;d.21 Oct 1962)

  sp: Nellie Jane CHARLTON (m.24 Mar 1946;d.25 Oct 1964)

    5. Joyce M. MONTI

      sp: Thomas A. BEISHIR

        6. James Joseph BEISHIR

        6. Paul Thomas BEISHIR

        6. Patrick Joseph BEISHIR

        6. Timothy Andrew BEISHIR

    5. JoAnn M. MONTI

    5. Unknown INFANT

    5. Sam MONTI Jr. (b.21 Oct 1950-St. Louis,MO;d.25 Oct 1950-St. Louis,MO)

4. Dominica (Babe) Marie MONTI (b.24 Apr 1919-St. Louis,MO;d.9 Oct 1986-Garside,Clark,Nevada)

  sp: Jack P. MARKU (b.29 Jun 1911;d.6 Jan 2004-Las Vegas,Clark Co.,NV)

  sp: Buck HENDRICKS (m.(Div))

  sp: Fred SYKES (m.(Div))

4. Sebastiano (Charles) Joseph MONTI Sr. (b.28 Nov 1920-St. Louis,MO;d.27 Jun 2006-St. Louis Co.,MO)

  sp: Milda Doris KAEMPFE (b.18 Mar 1925-Frohna,Perry Co.,MO;m.6 Jul 1946;d.13 Apr 2008-St. Louis Co., MO)

    5. Charles Joseph MONTI Jr

      sp: Vasana N. MALITONG-SIMON-CUNNINGHAM (m.17 Jul 1981)

        6. May Lynn (Cunningham) MONTI (adopted)

    5. Carmelo (Mel) Louis MONTI AIA

      sp: Mary Linda MILLER (m.1 Sep 1979)

        6. Jason Miller MONTI

    5. Michael James MONTI

      sp: Mary POLITTE-MCGOWAN (m.17 Aug 1974(Div))

        6. Candace Lee MONTI

        6. Michelle (McGowan) MONTI (adopted)

        6. Paul Michael (McGowan) MONTI (adopted)

    5. Paul Stephen MONTI

      sp: Ellen Marie VEIT (m.7 Aug 1976(Div))

        6. Victoria Lynn MONTI

        6. Stephen Paul MONTI

      sp: Marsha Lynn SUMNER-REAGAN (m.23 Jun 1990)

        6. Rebecca Lynn REAGAN

        6. Isaac David REAGAN

6. Sarah Beth REAGAN

6. Jacob Warren REAGAN

5. Sheila Christine MONTI

sp: Jose MOLINA (m.27 Dec 1985)

6. Molly MOLINA (stepdaughter)

5. Mark Edward MONTI

sp: Kathleen A. SCANLON (b.7 Oct 1960;m.11 Feb 1984(Div);d.4 Feb 2008-Affton,St. Louis Co.,MO)

6. Christopher Joseph MONTI

6. Kayla Christine MONTI

sp: Audra THOMAS (m.24 Apr 2007)

4. Frank (Little Frankie) Infant MONTI (b.15 Jun 1922-St. Louis,MO;d.11 Apr 1924-St. Louis,MO)

4. Francisco (Frank) Carmelo MONTI (b. 15 May 1924-St. Louis,MO;d.11Aug 2011-St. Louis Co.,MO)

sp: Glenness Faye BARBEE (m.5 Jul 1947)

5. Dr. Robert Louis MONTI

sp: Lyvia TOTH (m.1979)

6. Frank Nicholas MONTI

6. Ava Magdalena MONTI

5. Marilyn Frances MONTI

sp: William FARABEE (m.1980)

6. Angela Marie FARABEE

6. Erin Michelle FARABEE

5. Dr. Thomas Gerard MONTI

sp: Gina TURNER (m.(Div))

6. Sophia Faye MONTI

5. Infant MONTI (b.15 Dec 1953-Sts. Peter and Paul Cemetery,St. Louis,MO)

5. Infant 2nd MONTI (b.3 Dec 1957-Sts. Peter and Paul Cemetery,St. Louis,MO)

4. Rosario (Roy) Giuseppe MONTI (b.21 Feb 1926-St. Louis,MO;d.6 Apr 2011-St. Louis Co.,MO)

sp: Catherine Jane BANKER (m.28 Mar 1944;d.Jun 2011-St. Louis Co.,MO)

5. Roy Joseph MONTI II

sp: Wanda F. (?)

6. Roy Joseph MONTI III

6. Jackie MONTI

6. Theresa MONTI

6. Sam MONTI

6. Anthony MONTI

5. Catherine Mary MONTI (b.21 Oct 1948;d.29 Sep 1997)

sp: Dennis LEBEQUE

      6. Denise LEBEQUE

      6. Joseph Anthony (Joey) LEBEQUE (b.17 Sep 1976;d.24 Aug 1996)

    5. Marguerite Ann MONTI

     sp: Tom PALMER

      6. Augustina PALMER

      6. Tommy PALMER

      6. Anne PALMER

      6. Tobius PALMER

      6. Jill PALMER

  4. Veronica (Vera)  Mary MONTI

   sp: Leonard L. COMBREVIS (b.22 Mar 1928;m.7 May 1955;d.31 May 2005-St. Louis Co.,MO)

    5. Linda COMBREVIS

     sp: David GERHAUSER

      6. David GERHAUSER

      6. Shannon GERHAUSER

      6. Jason GERHAUSER

    5. Julia COMBREVIS

     sp: James HUGERICH

      6. Timmy HUGERICH

      6. Tina HUGERICH

    5. Leonard (Lenny) COMBREVIS

     sp: Chris LEISURE

      6. Tony COMBREVIS

    5. Louis COMBREVIS

    5. Jeffery COMBREVIS

    5. Vincent COMBREVIS

  4. Theresa MONTI (Died in infancy)

  4. Katherine MONTI (Died in infancy)

3. Pietro GIANINO (b.28 Jul 1894-Augusta,Siracusa,Sicily,Italy;d.24 Feb 1957-St. Louis,MO)

 sp: Leonarda D. DE LUCA (b.Abt 1891-Augusta,Siracusa,Sicily,Italy;m.Abt 1909 or 1912;d.Dec 1995-St.Louis,MO)

  4. Santa GIANINO (b.1912)

   sp: Oreste BIFFIGNANI (b.25 Apr 1905;d.Dec 1984)

    5. Joseph C. BIFFIGNANI (b.4 May 1932;d.5 May 2006)

     sp: Edna HOBUSCH

      6. Michael BIFFIGNANI

      6. Robert BIFFIGNANI

      6. Susan BIFFIGNANI

  5. Peter D. BIFFIGNANI

  5. Glenn O. BIFFIGNANI

  5. Frank L. BIFFIGNANI

 4. Frances GIANINO (b.1915;d.1998)

  sp: Charles KUEHNE (b.1921;d.1996)

 4. Carmelo GIANINO (b.1918;d.1992)

  sp: Edna MARTINEZ (b.1919;d.1996)

  5. Jackie GIANINO

  5. Carmello GIANINO

  5. Pete GIANINO

  5. Marco Michael GIANINO

  5. Ronnie GIANINO

  5. Darlene GIANINO

 4. Frank Ralph GIANINO (b.1921;d.Feb 2002-St. Louis,MO)

  sp: Frances Mary LAMARTINA

  5. Pete GIANINO

  5. Anthony GIANINO

  5. Frank GIANINO

  5. Leona GIANINO

 4. Sam GIANINO (b.27 Sep 1924-St. Louis,MO;d.15 Dec 1925-St. Louis,MO)

3. Salvatore Sam GIANINO (b.24 Oct 1895-Augusta,Siracusa,Sicily,Italy;d.28 Dec 1973-St. Louis,MO)

 sp: Wilma T. EISENHOFFER (b.14 Dec 1904;m.24 Dec 1923;d.Mar 1976-St. Louis,MO)

 4. Santa Theresa GIANINO (b.1928;d.1994)

  sp: Jacob Michael EGLER (b.1919;d.2002)

  5. James Michael EGLER

   sp: Deborah Jean BECKER (b.1953;d.2006)

   6. Jason M. EGLER

   6. Bryan J. EGLER

   6. Eric M. EGLER

   sp: Sharon Kay OGDEN

   6. Stephen James EDDINGTON

   6. Michelle Lynne BIANCHI

  5. Elizabeth Kay EGLER

   sp: Paul MALLMANN

   6. Paul MALLMANN

   6. Kelly MALLMANN

   6. Jessica MALLMANN

4. Carmelo GIANINO (b.6 Mar 1926;d.10 Jan 2010)

   sp: JoAnn FANETTI

   5. Donald Louis GIANINO

      sp: Ashley Lynn CHAMBERS

      6. Alyssa GIANINO

      6. Dominic GIANINO

   5. Anthony GIANINO

   sp: Shirley UNKNOWN

   5. Donald GIANINO

   5. Carmelo GIANINO

   5. Joyce GIANINO

   5. JoAnn GIANINO

   sp: Marian UNKNOWN

   5. Charles GIANINO

   5. Tina GIANINO

   sp: Barbara Jean MERTZ

   5. Salvatore (Sammy) GIANINO

4. Helen GIANINO (b.1931;d.1994)

   sp: Landis GEGG

   5. Landis R. GEGG

   5. Lynda S. GEGG

   5. William GEGG

   5. Donna M. GEGG

   5. Gerald GEGG

4. Thomas Joseph GIANINO (b.1934;d.1997)

   sp: Sharon Lee TIPTON (b.1937;d.2006)

   5. Daniel GIANINO

   5. Thomas GIANINO

   5. John GIANINO

4. Clementine GIANINO (b.1941;d.2005)

   sp: James Lee RENFROW (b.1937;d.1997)

   5. James Lee RENFROW

   5. Jeffery RENFROW

4. Roselee Marie GIANINO (b.1948;d.2006)

   sp: Michael FURHAM (b.1946;d.2001)

   5. Michael FURHAM

   5. John FURHAM

sp: Ronald A. CHRISTOPHER

   5. Ron CHRISTOPHER

   5. Denny CHRISTOPHER

3. Sebastiano Charles GIANINO (b.5 Nov 1898-Sicily,Italy;d.6 Aug 1979-St. Louis,MO)

  sp: Frances MIANO- MARCIANO (b.1906;m.3 Dec 1922;d.1995-St. Louis,MO)

   4. Carmelo GIANINO

    sp: Delores M. DUEWELL

     5. Gary S. GIANINO

      sp: Susan DOHACK

       6. Victoria GIANINO

       6. Nicholas GIANINO

       6. Valerie GIANINO

     5. Stephen C. GIANINO

      sp: Rebecca COX

       6. Sarah GIANINO

       6. Ruth GIANINO

       6. David GIANINO

       6. Daniel GIANINO

   4. Joseph GIANINO

    sp: Annette Frances KENNEDY

3. Ralph (formerly Alfio) GIANINO (b.20 Apr 1901-Augusta,Siracusa,Sicily,Italy;d.15 Jan 1986-St. Louis,MO)

  sp: Carolina V. MERLO (b.12 Oct 1909-St. Louis,MO;m.17 Aug 1928;d.Oct 1999-St. Louis,MO)

   4. Carolina GIANINO (b.20 Aug 1929-St. Louis,MO)

    sp: Bill BAYNES

   4. Carmelo Ralph GIANINO (b.25 Dec 1931-St. Louis,MO;d.May 1971-Missouri)

    sp: Barbara SINNWELL

     5. Ralph GIANINO

     5. Wallie GIANINO

     5. Rachelle GIANINO

     5. Michael GIANINO

     5. Anthony GIANINO

     5. Ann GIANINO

   4. Dolores GIANINO

   4. Louis GIANINO

    sp: Marilyn UNKNOWN

   4. Henry GIANINO

   4. Terry GIANINO

sp: Jim RAYFIELD

4. Maria GIANINO

    sp: Duwayne HALL

4. Charlene GIANINO

    sp: Bill HALL

3. Domenica Minnie GIANINO (b.29 Sep 1903-Augusta,Siracusa,Sicily,Italy;d.Jan 1984-St. Louis,MO)

    sp: Phillip VIRGA (b.1893;m.8 Aug 1927;d.Nov 1966-St. Louis,MO)

4. Carmello VIRGA

    sp: Rose KLEIN

    5. Beverly VIRGA

    5. Danny VIRGA

    5. Christopher VIRGA

4. Bertha VIRGA (b.1928;d.1979)

    sp: Albert T. FRATTINI (b.1921;d.1990)

    5. Gale J. FRATTINI

    5. Sandra D. FRATTINI

    5. Deborah A. FRATTINI

    5. Mary F. FRATTINI

4. Santa VIRGA

    sp: Luke DOLAN (b.1924;d.2006)

4. Joseph V. VIRGA (b.28 Jul 1929;d.3 Mar 1989)

    sp: Imogene GRAHAM

    5. Tony VIRGA

    5. Sara VIRGA

3. Marco Joseph GIUFFRIDA (fostered) (b.5 Oct 1894-Sicily,Italy;d.18 Feb 1958-St. Louis,MO)

**Three Generations at the
50th Wedding Anniversary Party for Eligio and Sebastiana Monti**
December 1, 1951

**Seated on Floor, Left to Right:** Donna Marie Monti, Joyce Monti, Catherine Mary Monti, Louis C. Monti, Joann Monti, Roy Monti Jr., Richard Willis III, and Dominic Monti

**Seated Behind Table, Left to Right:** Santa (Gianino) Gianino, Eligio Monti, Sebastiana (Gianino) Monti, and Milda (Kaempfe) Monti holding Charles Monti Jr.

**Standing Left to Right:** Francisco (Frank) Monti, Rosario (Roy) Monti, (hidden face Sammy Gianino), Dominic (Don) Monti, Maria (Mary) (Monti) Willis, Richard Willis, Dominica Marie (Babe) (Monti) Hendricks, Veronica (Vera) Monti, Josephine (Josie) (Monti) Gianino, Salvatore (Sam) Monti, Nellie Jane (Charlton) Monti, Theresa (Genoni) Monti, Joseph (Joe) Monti, Jane (?) Monti, Louis R. Monti, Sebastiano (Charles) Monti holding son Carmelo, Don Peel, Kathleen (Viviano) Peel, and Viola (Gutweiler) Gianino.

Photograph courtesy of Milda (Kaempfe) Monti Estate

# Bibliography

This Bibliography contains the resources that have been used to construct this genealogy and family history. I attempted to include every book, document, Internet website or person, but any omission of credit is purely unintentional and should not be construed as plagiarism or copyright infringement.

## Books

*American International Encyclopedia*, published by Little and Ives 1954

*Boston's West End* by Anthony Mitchell Sammarco, Arcadia Publishing 2001

*In the Line of Duty: St. Louis Police Officers Who Made the Ultimate Sacrifice* by Barbara Miksicek, Stephen Pollihan and David McElreath, published by Napsac Intl. 1991

*Lands and Peoples*, Vol. 2, P. 381, published by Grolier Society 1955

*New World History of Montis* published by Halbert's Family Heritage

*U.S.S. Block Island – CVE 21 and CVE 106 – United States Navy* published by Anchor Printing Corp.

## Documents, Microfilm and Records

"Alien Registration Forms" for Eligio Monti, Sebastiana (Gianino) Monti and Alfio Gianino dated 1940 from the U.S. Department of Justice, Immigration and Naturalization Service

Birth Record for Eligio Monte from Catania, Sicily provided by Victoria Monti

Catholic Cemeteries of the Archdiocese of St. Louis, MO, online burial records

City Directories for Boston, Mass. 1903 to 1925 (Microfilm)

Citizenship papers for Ralph (Alfio) Monti from U.S. Dept of Justice, Immigration and Naturalization Service

Cover, inside cover, page layout, and all graphic design by Mary Linda Miller © 2011

E-Mails or letters from Milda (Kaempfe) Monti, Sharon Egler, Charles Monti Jr., Paul Monti, Sheila Monti-Molina, Louis C. Monti, Robert Willis, Jill Palmer, Erin Farabee, Frank Monti, Roy Monti, Vera Monti, Tom and Joyce Beishir, and Debbie Hadican.

Death Certificates from Missouri for Milda Doris Monti, Charles Joseph Monti Sr., Eligio Louis Monti, Sebastiana (Anna) Monti, Carmelo Monti, Frank Monti, Sam Monti, Carmelo Gianino, Santa Gianino, Sebastiano Charles Gianino, Dominico Gianino, Giuseppa Josephine (Balsamo) Gianino, Eugene A. Kavanaugh, and Frank Munsil.

Descendants of Pietro Gianino – large descendants chart with Gianino family members March 2007 produced by Sharon Egler

Handwritten genealogy lists by Milda Monti, Carmelo L. Monti, Paul Monti, and Sheila Monti-Molina

Illustrations of Monte Etna and Trinacria by Carmelo L. Monti, 2009

Letter dated December 22, 1948 from Charles L. Monti to Mrs. Charles Monti, Box 36, Frohna, Missouri

Maps that were referenced: Italy by Rand McNally; Europe, National Geographic Magazine; Boston area from Boston West End; The Hill, as a portion of St. Louis, p. 37 from Wunnenberg's Street Guide 1993; Illinois and Missouri by Automobile Association of America

Maps of Sicily, Boston's West End, and The Hill in St. Louis, MO drawn by Carmelo L. Monti in 2003 and 2009

Marriage Record for Eligio Monte and Sebastiana Gianino dated Dec. 1, 1901 from Augusta, Sicily provided by Victoria Monti

Newspaper article in the *St. Louis Globe Democrat*
> "Youth Slain, Father and Patrolman Shot in Duel" June 18, 1933, page 1-6, Part One (Four photographs and headlines reproduced herein)

Newspaper articles in the *St. Louis Post-Dispatch*
> "Youth Killed, Two Shot, In Family Fight With Police" June 18, 1933, p. 1-3, Part One (Three photographs with a portion of p. 3 and headlines reproduced herein)
> Tim Bryant, "87-Year-Old With Grudge Charged in Hill Killing" Sept. 17, 1994, p. 1A.
> Bill Bryan, "The 38-Year Story Behind a Killing" Sept. 25, 1994, p. 1A.
> Dave Dorr, "Up and Down The Hill" Oct. 23, 1994, p. 1C.

Newspaper article in the *South County Journal*
> Julie Randle "Veteran Recalls Sinking of Carrier" May 26, 2004, p. B-1

Photographs from the collection of Mary Miller and Carmelo L. Monti include Monti Headstone; 5242 Wilson Avenue; and Sam Monti in Army uniform

Photograph of the author Mary Linda Miller by Carmelo L. Monti, AIA 2009

Photographs from the collection of Rob Willis include Carmelo Monti c. 1920s; group photo of Monti family gathering circa 1955-1960; and group photo of Charles Monti Sr. in sailor uniform with his parents 1943.

Photographs from the Milda (Kaempfe) Monti Estate provided by Sheila Monti Molina include: Monti-Gianino family portrait 1922-23; Eligio and Sebastiana Monti c. 1922; group with Monti family c. 1930s; group with Santa Gianino, Eligio Monti and Sebastiana Monti 1951 (also divided for this book into individual portraits); group with Gianino and Monti family members 1951 for 50th Wedding Anniversary; group at Frank Monti's wedding reception 1947; Carmelo Monti c. 1920s; Charles Monti Sr. in Navy uniform; group with Charles, Vera and Sam Monti and Kathleen and Mary (Monti) Viviano; and a second group with Gianino and Monti family members 1951 for 50th Wedding Anniversary. (Note that "head-shot" photos of some Monti siblings were cropped from either the 1930s era or the 1947 Monti group photos.)

Photograph of Ellis Island: Library of Congress, Prints and Photographs Division, Washington, D.C. 20540 USA cph 3a40441 http://hdl.loc.gov/loc.pnp/cph.3a40441 Ca. 1913, View of Ellis Island NY looking across water

Photographs: Hale Street, Boston MA 1954 courtesy of West End Historical Association (Cropped versions of these photos can also be found in Anthony Sammarco's book *Boston's West End* on page 52.)

Photograph of Frank Monti in Coast Guard uniform c. 1943 courtesy of Frank Monti via Erin Farabee

Photograph of Veronica Monti in front of 4131 Flad Avenue 1941 courtesy of Veronica (Monti) Combrevis

Photograph of Roy Monti courtesy of Roy Monti

Photographs of the headstone for Carmelo and Santa (Gianino) Gianino in Sts. Peter and Paul Cemetery, St. Louis, Missouri courtesy of Katie of Findagrave.com

Ship's Manifest Records from Ellis Island Foundation, Inc. (Eligio Monti and various Gianino)

Ship's Manifest Records from National Archives (Sebastiana Gianino Monti)

1910 Census for Missouri (Microfilm and HeritageQuest)

1920 Census for Missouri (Microfilm, Ancesty.com, and HeritageQuest)

1930 Census for Missouri (Microfilm, Ancestry. Com, and Robert Willis)

## Other Resources

Boston Library, Main Branch, Boston, Massachusetts
Ellis Island Foundation (membership)
Latter Day Saints Genealogy Library, Winter Park, Florida
Library of Congress American Memory Online Collection
Missouri Bureau of Vital Statistic, Jefferson City, Missouri
Missouri State Archives, Jefferson City, Missouri
Orange County Public Library, Main Branch, Orlando, Florida
PAF5 (Personal Ancestral File 5th generation) software from familysearch.org
St. Louis City Library, Main Branch, St. Louis, Missouri

## Internet Websites

One website in particular played a major role: familysearch.org. It is operated by the Latter Day Saints (Mormon) and was invaluable because of its vast resources and broad spectrum of coverage, and it provided the free software program PAF5, which generated the "Descendants of Pietro Gianino" chart. Most websites were first visited in 2003 and some have ceased to exist since then.

## General

www.familysearch.org
www.rootsweb.com
www.sos.state.mo.us/arc
www.maps.google.com/maps
www.multimap.com
www.mapquest.com
www.hamrick.com/names/
www.surnames.behindthename.com/
www.ssdi.rootsweb.ancestry.com/
www.findagrave.com/
www.catalog.loc.gov/
www.ocls.info

## Monti-Gianino

www.ellisislandrecords.org
www.ancestorhunt.com/ellis_island_photos.html
www.archstl.org/cemeteries/
www.archstl.org/cemeteries/
www.boris.vulcanoetna.com/gifs/image/flowmaps/1381_1669.jpg
www.boris.vulcanoetna.com/ETNA_erupt1.html
www.boris.vulcanoetna.com/ETNA_elencold.html
www.eurotravelling.net/italy/catania_sicily/catania_sicily_history.htm
www.initaly.com/regions/sicily/history.htm
www.amicasicilia.it/cultura/storia-eng.htm
www.initaly.com/regions/sicily/giovvrga.htm
www.freepages.genealogy.rootsweb.com/~torchia/names/italiannames.htm
www.sicilia.indettaglio.it/eng/cognomi/motore/motore.html

www.sicilia.indettaglio.it/eng/comuni/sr/augusta/augusta.html
www.sicilia.indettaglio.it/eng/comuni/ct/catania/catania.html
www.bestofsicily.com/genealogy.html
www.bestofsicily.com/religion.htm
www.italyworldclub.com/genealogy/surnames/g.htm
www.memory.loc.gov/ammem/browse/ListSome.php?category=Immigration,
        +American%20Expansion
www.www.sizilien-rad.de/
www.volcano.oregonstate.edu/volcanoes/etna/index.html
www.creationwiki.org/Sicily
www.sights.seindal.dk/sight/613_Trinacria.html
www.bellanti.org/Sicily.htm
www.ninniradicini.it/articoli/trinacria_sicily_history_mythology.htm
www.stlouis.missouri.org/neighborhoods/history/thehill/text13.htm
www.wikitravel.org/en/St_Louis
www.washingtonmo.com/1904/index.htm
www.en.wikipedia.org/wiki/Kansas_City_Chiefs
www.en.wikipedia.org/wiki/Tonopah_Test_Range
www.stlcin.missouri.org/history/structdetail.cfm?Master_ID=1945
www.falstaffbrewing.com/carling-.htm
www.stlouis.missouri.org/citygov/refuse/
www.en.wikipedia.org/wiki/Old_St._Charles_Bridge
www.ranken.edu/
www.kennedyking.ccc.edu/about_history.asp
www.foundersaffton.org/
www.wikipedia.org/wiki/Prohibition_in_the_United_States
www.stltoday.com/help/archives/simplesearch
www.nl.newsbank.com
www.casalomaballroom.com/
www.everysport.net/GamePlan3/Default.aspx?alias=everysport.net/GamePlan3/SCLParish
www.wikipedia.org/wiki/Battle_of_Monte_Cassino
www.en.wikipedia.org/wiki/Seventh_United_States_Army
www.stlfire4.loudclick.net/
www.kaboodle.com/reviews/chuck-berry-biography
www.geocities.com/chuckberryinfo/
www.stlouis.missouri.org/greaterville/history.htm
www.slpl.lib.mo.us/libsrc/m-street.htm
www.stlouis.missouri.org/neighborhoods/history/arlington/hospitals1.htm
www.satchelpaige.com/bio2.html
www.youtube.com/watch?v=w_Bd5-APPBw
www.wikipedia.org/wiki/Yogi_Berra
www.en.wikipedia.org/wiki/Joe_Garagiola,_Sr
www.en.wikipedia.org/wiki/Victor_Emanuel_III

# Proper Name Index

BALSANO (or BALSAMO), Giuseppa (Josephine) — 10, 49, 50, 63
BANKER, Catherine Jane — 45 - 47, 56
BARBEE, Glenness Faye — 56
BAYNES, Bill — 60
BECKER, Deborah Jean — 58
BEISHIR, James Joseph — 55
BEISHIR, Patrick Joseph — 55
BEISHIR, Paul Thomas — 55
BEISHIR, Thomas A — 39, 55, 63
BEISHIR, Timothy Andre — 55
BERRA, Lawrence (Yogi) — 41, 42
BERRY, Charles Edward Anderson (Chuck) — 28, 29
BERRY, Henry — 28
BERRY, Martha — 28
BIANCHI, Michelle Lynne — 58
BIFFIGNANI, Frank L. — 58
BIFFIGNANI, Glenn O. — 58
BIFFIGNANI, Joseph C. — 57
BIFFIGNANI, Michael — 57
BIFFIGNANI, Oreste — 57
BIFFIGNANI, Peter D. — 58
BIFFIGNANI, Robert — 57
BIFFIGNANI, Susan — 57
CHAMBERS, Ashley Lynn — 59
CHARLTON, Nellie Jane — 39, 40, 55, 62
CHRISTOPHER, Denny — 60
CHRISTOPHER, Ron — 60
CHRISTOPHER, Ronald A — 60
COMBREVIS, Jeffery — 47, 57
COMBREVIS, Julia — 47, 57
COMBREVIS, Leonard (Lenny) — 47, 48, 57
COMBREVIS, Leonard L. — 47, 57
COMBREVIS, Linda — 47, 48, 57
COMBREVIS, Louis — 47, 57
COMBREVIS, Tony — 47, 57
COMBREVIS, Vincent — 47, 57
COX, Rebecca — 60
DANIELE, Sebastiana — 9, 10, 18, 49, 50, 53
DE LUCA, Leonarda D. — 9,14, 57
DOHACK, Susan — 60
DOLAN, Luke — 61
DUEWELL, Delores M. — 60

EDDINGTON, Stephen James — 58
EGLER, Bryan J. — 58
EGLER, Elizabeth Kay — 58
EGLER, Eric M. — 58
EGLER, Jacob Michael — 58
EGLER, James Michael — 58
EGLER, Jason M — 58
EISENHOFFER, Wilma T. — 58
FANETTI, JoAnn — 59
FARABEE, Angela Marie — 56
FARABEE, Erin Michelle — 56, 63, 64
FARABEE, William — 56
FRATTINI, Albert T. — 61
FRATTINI, Deborah A. — 61
FRATTINI, Gale J. — 61
FRATTINI, Mary F. — 61
FRATTINI, Sandra D. — 61
FURHAM, John — 59
FURHAM, Michael (b. 1946) — 59
FURHAM, Michael — 59
GARAGIOLA, Joe — 41, 42
GEGG, Donna M. — 59
GEGG, Gerald — 59
GEGG, Landis — 59
GEGG, Landis R. — 59
GEGG, Lynda S. — 59
GEGG, William — 59
GENONI, Theresa — 31, 32, 53, 62
GERHAUSER, David — 57
GERHAUSER, David — 57
GERHAUSER, Jason — 57
GERHAUSER, Shannon — 57
GIANINO, Alyssa — 59
GIANINO, Ann — 60
GIANINO, Anthony — 58
GIANINO, Anthony — 59
GIANINO, Anthony — 60
GIANINO, Carmello — 58
GIANINO, Carmelo (b. 1865) — 3, 4, 9, 10, 13, 14, 17, 18, 19, 30, 34, 36, 50, 51, 53, 63, 64
GIANINO, Carmelo (b. 1918) — 58
GIANINO, Carmelo (b. 1926) — 59
GIANINO, Carmelo — 59
GIANINO, Carmelo — 60
GIANINO, Carmelo Ralph — 60

GIANINO, Carolina — 60
GIANINO, Charlene — 61
GIANINO, Charles — 59
GIANINO, Clementine — 59
GIANINO, Daniel — 59
GIANINO, Daniel — 60
GIANINO, Darlene — 58
GIANINO, David — 60
GIANINO, Dolores — 60
GIANINO, Domenica Minnie — 9, 17, 61
GIANINO, Dominic — 52
GIANINO, Dominic — 53
GIANINO, Dominic — 59
GIANINO, Dominico — 10, 63
GIANINO, Donald — 59
GIANINO, Donald Louis — 59
GIANINO, Frances — 58
GIANINO, Frank — 58
GIANINO, Frank Ralph — 58
GIANINO, Gary S. — 60
GIANINO, Helen — 59
GIANINO, Henry — 60
GIANINO, Jackie — 58
GIANINO, JoAnn — 59
GIANINO, John— 53
GIANINO, John— 59
GIANINO, Joseph — 60
GIANINO, Joyce — 59
GIANINO, Leona — 58
GIANINO, Louis — 53
GIANINO, Louis — 60
GIANINO, Marco Michael — 58
GIANINO, Maria — 61
GIANINO, Michael — 60
GIANINO, Nicholas — 60
GIANINO, Paula — 53
GIANINO, Pete — 58
GIANINO, Pete — 58
GIANINO, Pietro (b. 1894) — 8, 9, 13, 14, 23, 57
GIANINO, Pietro — 10, 18, 53, 63, 65
GIANINO, Rachelle — 60
GIANINO, Ralph — 60
GIANINO, Ralph (formerly Alfio) — 9, 17, 20, 23, 36, 60, 63
GIANINO, Rebecca — 53
GIANINO, Ronnie — 58

GIANINO, Roselee Marie — 59
GIANINO, Ruth — 60
GIANINO, Salvatore (Sam) (b. 1895) — 36, 58
GIANINO, Salvatore (Sammy) — 32, 46, 59, 62
GIANINO, Sam — 53
GIANINO, Sam — 53
GIANINO, Sam (b. 1924) — 58
GIANINO, Santa (b. 1866) — 3, 4, 9, 10, 17 - 20, 23, 25, 30, 50, 52,
        53, 62, 63, 64
GIANINO, Santa (b. 1912) — 9, 14, 57
GIANINO, Santa Theresa — 58
GIANINO, Santo — 28, 29, 32, 33, 53
GIANINO, Sarah — 60
GIANINO, Sebastiana — 3, 4 , 6 - 11, 16, 17, 20, 22 - 38, 43, 47, 50,
        51, 53, 62, 63, 64
GIANINO, Sebastiano Charles — 8, 9, 10, 17, 20, 51, 52, 60, 63
GIANINO, Stephen — 53
GIANINO, Stephen C. — 60
GIANINO, Terry — 60
GIANINO, Theresa — 53
GIANINO, Thomas — 59
GIANINO, Thomas Joseph — 59
GIANINO, Tina — 59
GIANINO, Valerie — 60
GIANINO, Victoria — 60
GIANINO, Wallie — 60
GIUFFRIDA, Marco Joseph (fostered) — 61
GRAHAM, Imogene — 61
GUTWEILER, Viola — 46, 53, 62
HADICAN, Thomas M. — 53
HALL, Bill — 61
HALL, Duwayne — 61
HAND, Shirley J. — 54
HARMON, Sandy Ellen — 54
HENDRICKS, Buck — 40, 55
HOBUSCH, Edna — 57
HUGERICH, James — 57
HUGERICH, Timmy — 57
HUGERICH, Tina — 57
JACOBI, Mark — 54
KAEMPFE, Milda Doris — 39, 42 - 44, 55, 62, 63
KENNEDY, Annette Frances — 60
KENNETT, Chelsea — 54
KENNETT, Michael — 54
KENNETT, Michael — 54

KENNETT, Richard — 54

KLEIN, Rose — 61

KUEHNE, Charles — 58

LAMARTINA, Frances Mary — 58

LEBEQUE, Denise — 57

LEBEQUE, Dennis — 56

LEBEQUE, Joseph Anthony (Joey) — 57

LEISURE, Chris — 57

MALITONG-SIMON-CUNNINGHAM, Vasana — 55

MALLMANN, Jessica — 58

MALLMANN, Kelly — 58

MALLMANN, Paul — 58

MALLMANN, Paul — 58

MARKU, Jack P. — 40, 55

MARTINEZ, Edna — 58

MERLO, Carolina V. — 60

MERTZ, Barbara Jean — 59

MIANO- MARCIANO, Frances — 60

MILLER, Mary Linda — 13, 55, 63, 64, 71, 72

MOLINA, Jose — 56

MOLINA, Molly — 56

MONTE, Eligio Luigi — See MONTI, Eligio Louis

MONTI, Anthony — 56

MONTI, Arturo Gianino — 4, 8, 17, 27, 30, 31, 51, 53

MONTI, Ava Magdalena — 56

MONTI, Candace Lee — 55

MONTI, Carmelo (b. 1913) — 11, 28, 29, 34 - 37, 51, 54, 63, 64

MONTI, Carmelo (Mel) Louis AIA (b. 1948) — 1, 13, 14, 40, 41, 46, 51, 55, 62, 63, 64, 75, 76

MONTI, Catherine Mary — 46, 56, 62

MONTI, Charles Joseph Sr. (b. 1920) — See MONTI, Sebastiano (Charles) Joseph

MONTI, Charles Joseph Jr. (b. 1947) — 55, 62, 63

MONTI, Christopher Joseph — 56

MONTI, Deborah J. — 53, 63

MONTI, Diane — 53

MONTI, Domenic — 54

MONTI, Domenic Jospeh Jr. — 54, 62

MONTI, Dominic (Don) Joseph — 11, 16, 25, 26, 28, 30 - 39, 51, 54, 62

MONTI, Dominica (Babe) Marie — 11, 16, 25, 26, 28, 30 - 36, 39 - 41, 47, 55, 62

MONTI, Donna — 54

MONTI, Donna Marie — 53, 62

MONTI, Eligio Louis — 3 - 11, 13, 14, 16, 17, 20 - 37, 43, 44, 47, 49 - 51, 53, 62, 63, 64

MONTI, Francisco (Frank) Carmelo — 16, 25, 26, 28, 30, 31, 36, 44, 45, 51, 56, 62, 63, 64

MONTI, Frank Infant (Little Frankie) — 24, 30, 44, 56, 63
MONTI, Frank Nicholas — 56
MONTI, Infant — 56
MONTI, Infant 2nd — 56
MONTI, Jackie — 56
MONTI, Jason Miller — 55
MONTI, JoAnn M. — 39, 40, 55, 62
MONTI, Joseph (Joe) Louis — 11, 16, 17, 25, 26, 31, 32, 53, 62
MONTI, Josephine (Josie) Theresa — 11, 16, 25, 26, 28 - 33, 38, 53, 62
MONTI, Joyce M. — 39, 40, 55, 62, 63
MONTI, Katherine (Infant) — 30, 57
MONTI, Kayla Christine — 56
MONTI, Lisa — 54
MONTI, Louis Carmelo — 28, 31, 32, 34, 37, 38, 40, 41, 51, 54, 62, 63
MONTI, Louis R. — 53, 62
MONTI, Marguerite Ann — 57
MONTI, Maria (Mary) Margaret — 11, 16, 25, 26, 28, 30 - 33, 41, 53, 62, 64
MONTI, Marilyn Frances — 56
MONTI, Mark Edward — 56
MONTI, May Lynn (Cunningham) — 55
MONTI, Michael James — 55
MONTI, Michelle (McGowan) — 55
MONTI, Paul Michael (McGowan) — 55
MONTI, Paul Stephen — 55, 63
MONTI, Robert Louis, Dr. — 56
MONTI, Rosario (Roy) Giuseppe — 16, 25, 26, 28, 30, 31, 34, 36, 39,
            44 - 47, 56, 62, 63, 64
MONTI, Roy Joseph II — 56, 62
MONTI, Roy Joseph III — 56
MONTI, Salvatore (Sam) Joseph Arturo — 11, 16, 25, 26, 28, 30, 31, 36 - 42,
            46, 51, 55, 62, 63, 64
MONTI, Sam — 56
MONTI, Sam Jr. (b. 1950) — 39, 40, 55
MONTI, Sebastiano (Charles) Joseph — 16, 20, 25, 26, 28 - 31, 33, 37 - 39,
            41 - 46, 55, 62, 63, 64
MONTI, Sheila Christine — 1, 31, 42, 56, 63, 64
MONTI, Sophia Faye — 56
MONTI, Stephen Paul — 55
MONTI, Theresa — 56
MONTI, Theresa (Infant) — 30, 57
MONTI, Thomas Gerard Dr. — 56
MONTI, Veronica (Vera) Mary — 16, 25, 26, 28, 29, 32, 34, 38-41, 47,
            48, 57, 62, 63, 64
MONTI, Victoria Lynn — 55, 63
MONTI, Vincent — 54

OGDEN, Sharon Kay — 20, 58, 63
PALMER, Anne — 57
PALMER, Augustina — 57
PALMER, Jill — 57, 63
PALMER, Tobius — 57
PALMER, Tom — 57
PALMER, Tommy — 57
PEEL, Debbie — 54
PEEL, Don — 54, 62
PEEL, Gary — 54
PEEL, Sandra — 54
POLITTE-MCGOWAN, Mary — 55
RAYFIELD, Jim — 61
REAGAN, Isaac David — 55
REAGAN, Jacob Warren — 56
REAGAN, Rebecca Lynn — 55
REAGAN, Sarah Beth — 56
RENFROW, James Lee (b. 1937) — 59
RENFROW, James Lee — 59
RENFROW, Jeffery — 59
SCANLON, Kathleen A. — 44, 56
SCHMITT, Darlyn — 53
SCHMITT, Denise — 53
SCHMITT, Ed — 53
SCHMITT, Joey — 53
SIMS, Lona Bernice — 37, 38, 54
SINNWELL, Barbara — 60
SMITH, Robert — 54
SUM, Mary Stephanie — 53
SUMNER-REAGAN, Marsha Lynn — 55
SYKES, Fred — 40, 55
THOMAS, Audra — 56
TIPTON, Sharon Lee — 59
TOTH, Lyvia — 56
TURNER, Gina — 56
VEIT, Ellen Marie — 55
VICTOR EMMANUEL III — 4, 23
VIRGA, Bertha — 61
VIRGA, Beverly — 61
VIRGA, Carmello — 61
VIRGA, Christopher — 61
VIRGA, Danny — 61
VIRGA, Joseph V. — 61
VIRGA, Phillip — 61
VIRGA, Santa — 61

VIRGA, Sara — 61
VIRGA, Tony — 61
VIVIANO, Anthony Jr. — 33, 53
VIVIANO, Anthony Sr. — 33
VIVIANO, Kathleen — 33, 41, 54, 64
WILLIS, Adair — 54
WILLIS, Karrie K. — 54
WILLIS, Keith J. — 54
WILLIS, Kevin E. — 54
WILLIS, Kraig L. — 54
WILLIS, Krista K. — 54
WILLIS, Monica — 54
WILLIS, Monte S. Jr. — 54
WILLIS, Monte Scott — 54
WILLIS, Richard Lee III — 33, 54, 62
WILLIS, Richard Lee Jr. — 33, 54, 62
WILLIS, Robert Lee — 10, 33, 54, 63, 64
WILLIS, Ronda Lynn — 33, 54

# About the Author

Reared in St. Louis, Missouri, Mary Linda Miller graduated *summa cum laude* with a Bachelor of Fine Arts degree from Maryville University in 1978; worked for twenty-five years doing design, drafting, and technical writing in the fields of civil engineering and architecture while living in St. Louis, Phoenix, and Kaneohe, Hawaii; and traveled extensively in the United States, Western Europe, and Japan. She currently resides in Orlando, Florida with her husband of over thirty years Carmelo L. Monti, AIA, who is a descendant of Eligio and Sebastiana (Gianino) Monti.

Her writing includes poetry; a technical manual for interpreting American with Disabilities Act Design Standards for the Hawaiian State Commission on Persons with Disabilities; a technical manual for corporate civil engineering AutoCAD drafting standards written in Phoenix; three other self-published books of genealogy and family history; and a children's early chapter book *Terry Trackhoe Goes Missing* that was illustrated by husband Carmelo Monti. She also participated with a group of online writers and poets in producing three anthologies of poetry and short stories.

Works in progress include a completed novel *Liminality: The Fox Woman's Child*, which combines Japanese mythology and religion with mid-20th-century American history for which she seeks representation; an unfinished sequel *Terry Trackhoe Goes Swimming*; and an unfinished novel that combines the Hawaiian mythological romance of Laieikawai with a modern event—Hurricane Iniki—which she experienced first-hand while living on Oahu. Hurricane Charley, which ripped through Orlando in 2004, reinforced that experience, and every hurricane season in Florida reminds her that she still has a story to tell.

# Books by the Author

*The Genealogy of Carmelo Louis Monti and His Ancestral History*
   (Limited edition and out of print)

*The Family History and Genealogy of*
*Mollie Camalene Eads and Pearl Marion Tipton*
   (Limited edition and out of print)

*A Farm Near Frohna:*
   *The Story Behind a Missouri Century Farm*
   *Kaempfe-Koenig Family History and Genealogy*

*Terry Trackhoe Goes Missing*

*An Hour Over Denali*
   *Photography by Mary Linda Miller and Carmelo L. Monti, AIA*

# Anthologies with the Author's Work

*Rambling Poets at Café Cyber Volume I*

*Poeticising Chat – Rambling Poets at Café Cyber Volume II*

*Rainbow Lights Ablaze*

**Visit her websites for more information**
**www.marylindamiller.com**
**www.terrytrackhoe.com**

# Add Your Own Notes

Made in the USA
Las Vegas, NV
28 October 2021